4

25 COMMON CORE MATH LESSONS
for the Interactive Whiteboard

Ready-to-Use, Animated PowerPoint® Lessons With Leveled Practice Pages
That Help Students Learn and Review Key Common Core Math Concepts

by Steve Wyborney

New York ◦ Toronto ◦ London ◦ Auckland ◦ Sydney
New Delhi ◦ Mexico City ◦ Hong Kong ◦ Buenos Aires

Teaching Resources

For Ben, with great love and admiration.
You surpass me.

About the CD The PowerPoint files in the attached CD are in .ppsx format. They can be opened with PowerPoint 2007 or later. If your PC does not have PowerPoint, you can download and install the free PowerPoint Viewer, which allows you to view full-featured presentations created in PowerPoint 97 and later versions.

Editor: Maria L. Chang
Cover design by Scott Davis
Interior design by Grafica Inc.

ISBN: 978-0-545-48619-4
Copyright © 2014 by Steve Wyborney
All rights reserved.
Printed in the U.S.A.

1 2 3 4 5 6 7 8 9 10   40   20 19 18 17 16 15 14

Table of Contents

The numbers in parentheses refer to corresponding PowerPoint lessons on the CD.

Welcome to *25 Common Core Math Lessons for the Interactive Whiteboard*!

The landscape around mathematical instruction is rapidly changing. Thanks to the Common Core State Standards, students and educators will learn and experience mathematical content in a different way. Many educators, schools, and districts are beginning new journeys in response to these changes and are seeking new resources—perhaps the reason you now have this book in your hands. It is my hope that this book will be a vital, powerful resource in your classroom.

This unique resource combines ready-to-use PowerPoint® lessons for your interactive whiteboard with reproducible, leveled practice sheets. The lessons place you, the classroom teacher, squarely at the center of the resource. I am certain you will feel that when you begin using it. This resource empowers you during the instructional sequence by providing visual prompts, animations, questions, and response/feedback opportunities that are completely paced by you.

The purposeful animation in the lessons is designed to make the math concepts listed in the standards more accessible to students. I fully recognize that animation can provide either clarity or distraction. For this reason, these lessons have been carefully crafted so that the animation works to simplify and illuminate mathematical concepts that students might otherwise find difficult to understand.

Thank you for including *25 Common Core Math Lessons for the Interactive Whiteboard* among your resources. I know that the resources we all treasure are the ones that make our lives simpler and our students' learning clearer. That is exactly what I believe this resource will be for you.

Kind regards,

Steve Wyborney

How to Use This Book

25 Common Core Math Lessons for the Interactive Whiteboard has been designed with whole-class instruction in mind; however, the lessons can also be used with individual students or with small groups.

This book features 25 PowerPoint lessons that support the Common Core State Standards for Mathematics. Each lesson is animated to bring clarity to a particular standard. While every lesson is complete, you might find it useful to go back and focus on a portion of a lesson to explore a particular question in greater depth. You can also use the lessons to preview upcoming content before teaching. Some of the strategies within the lessons may be new to you. In that case, they may serve as part of your personal professional learning journey.

Animated Lessons

The lessons in the attached CD are multi-click animation sequences that introduce standards-based math skills and concepts, such as finding factor pairs, rounding whole numbers, multiplying 2-digit numbers, adding, subtracting, and multiplying fractions, identifying angles, and more. **The file names on the CD correspond to the numbers next to the lesson titles on the table of contents.** For example, 4.001.ppsx features the lesson "Understanding Multiplication," 4.002.ppsx is "Divisibility Test for 3," and so on. Simply pop the CD into your computer and open the desired lesson with PowerPoint. For whole-class instruction, connect your computer to the interactive whiteboard or to a projector in front of a blank screen.

As you click (or otherwise advance) through a PowerPoint lesson and watch the animation unfold, you will find many opportunities to direct questions to your students. In general, each lesson advances from simpler, foundational concepts toward more complex concepts. Likewise, the pacing of the lesson also increases from beginning to end.

Since teacher mobility can sometimes be limited when using interactive whiteboards, I recommend that you acquire some type of presentation remote to advance the animations. Having a presentation remote will allow you to move easily throughout your classroom during instruction. If you don't have one, you can still use your interactive whiteboard or a wireless mouse.

The Script

Each lesson comes with a running script at the bottom of the screen. (The CD also contains a printable version of each script as a PDF file.) You can use the script in many different ways. One option is to read the script as you click through the lesson. The text has been carefully timed to correlate with the lesson's purposeful animation. Of course, you may also opt not to use the script at all, choosing to use different phrasing from what's in the lesson.

You can also use the script as a guide to help you prepare for the lesson content. As you preview the lesson, you can read through the script to better understand the timing of the animation as well as the sequence and pacing of the lesson. I predict you will use the script at some points and then veer away from it at other points where you sense opportunities for more in-depth conversations with your students.

Later, students who might benefit from a review could go through the lessons on their own—individually, in pairs, or in small groups. Simply sit them in front of a computer and allow them to click through the slideshow at their own pace, using the script to help them recall the lesson.

TIP

Before presenting a lesson to the whole class, review it a few times so you can see the progression of the lesson and read the script.

Lightning Round and Closing Question

Some lessons include a Lightning Round near the end of the slideshow. The slides in this section are marked by a lightning bolt and function in a similar way to flash cards. The Lightning Round indicates that the lesson has reached a point where your students should be able to respond quickly to a given question. When you see the lightning bolt, the next click will generally present the question, and the click after that will present the answer. What happens in between those two clicks is the most important part of this round. At that point, you might ask students for predictions and explanations, guide them toward validating their reasoning, layer in additional questions, or connect content with students' lives. The last slide of each lesson features a Closing Question, which is essentially a review of the concept to ensure that students fully understand the lesson.

TIP

In some versions of PowerPoint, a popup toolbar may appear at the bottom left of the screen during a slideshow presentation. This toolbar is generally useful for navigating from slide to slide, but the pen, in particular, can come in handy if you want to write annotations on the screen to explain a concept further or show your work.

If the toolbar does not automatically appear on your slideshow, you can activate it by going to "PowerPoint Options," selecting "Advanced," then checking "Show popup toolbar" underneath "Slide show." (On a Mac, go to "PowerPoint Preferences," click on the "View" tab, then choose "Pop-up menu button" on the drop-down menu next to "Slide show navigation.")

Common Core Content Indicators

On every lesson, you will find indicators that reference specific Common Core State Standards for Mathematics. None of the lessons are intended to provide a comprehensive definition of any of the standards; however, they are all centered squarely on specific standards, which can be referenced by looking at the lower-right corner of the lesson's title page. For a list of all the lessons and the standards they meet, see page 8.

Reproducible Practice Pages

This book contains reproducible worksheets so students can practice their new skills independently, with a partner or small group, or as a whole class. Each lesson comes with three practice pages at levels A (below grade level), B (at grade level), and C (above grade level). While you can distribute the sheets according to students' abilities, you could also give students all three sheets at different times to reinforce the skills and concepts learned from the lesson. Use the sheets for homework, independent in-class work, practice, or review. An answer key is provided at the end of the book.

The Teacher's Role

Each lesson has been purposefully designed to connect students to the content through the teacher. This is not an electronic resource that minimizes the role of the teacher. In contrast, the instruction runs directly through you, as it should. No one knows your students better than you. Although each lesson is complete and can be taught as listed, I strongly believe that some of the best instructional opportunities will happen when you pause the lesson and pursue a question or opportunity that has been revealed. In the moments when you say, "That's an interesting question. What do you think?" or "Can you explain your thinking?" or "What is another way to think about this?" you will find excellent opportunities to guide your students toward successful and powerful mathematical learning.

Lesson Overview

Below is a list of the 25 PowerPoint lessons you'll find on the CD, including a summary and the Common Core State Standard each lesson meets. For a full description of the standards, see page 13.

4.001 Understanding Multiplication (4.OA.A.1)

With some visual help on a multiplication table and a number line, students understand that "5 times as many as 7" is another way of saying 5 × 7.

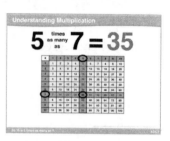

4.002 Divisibility Test for 3 (4.OA.B.4)

In this lesson, students learn a key strategy for finding out if a number is divisible by 3: They add the digits of the number and see if the sum of its digits is divisible by 3.

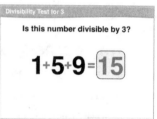

4.003 Finding Factor Pairs (4.OA.B.4)

Students list all the factor pairs of a number, starting with 1 and the number itself. They then proceed to the next number, 2, to see if it is a factor and, if so, determine its partner. As they continue to test each succeeding number, students learn to stop when they reach a factor that has been found already, or, if the number is a square, when they have identified all the factors up to the square root.

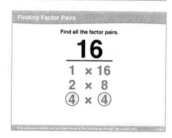

4.004 Place Value & Expanded Form (4.NBT.A.1, 4.NBT.A.2)

Given a single digit, students identify its value based upon its place; for example, the value of the digit 4 in the thousands place is 4,000. With this knowledge, they then learn to write a number in expanded form; for example, 4,286 = 4,000 + 200 + 80 + 6.

4.005 Comparing Numbers (4.NBT.A.2)

Students compare large numbers by first aligning the places of each number, then comparing each place value, starting with the left-most digit, until they find the place where the digits are different. They then determine whether the first number is greater than, less than, or equal to the second number.

4.006 Rounding Whole Numbers (4.NBT.A.3)

To round a number to the nearest ten, students identify the digit in the tens place and how many tens are in the number. They then look at the digit to the right. If the digit is 5 or more, they round up. Otherwise, they round down. Students apply the same strategy to round to the nearest hundred and the nearest thousand, always focusing on the place value called for and the digit to its right. For example, to round 6,487 to the nearest hundred, they look at the digit in the hundreds place *(4)* and determine how many hundreds are in the number *(64)*. They then look at the digit to the right of 4 *(8)* and decide to round up because the number is greater than 5. So, the nearest hundred is 6,500.

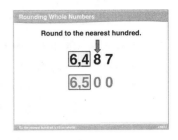

4.007 Adding Multi-Digit Whole Numbers (4.NBT.B.4)

In this lesson, students learn how to add six-digit numbers in columns. They first add the digits in the ones column, then the digits in the tens column, then the digits in the hundreds, and so on. Problems progress from addition with no regrouping to addition with regrouping.

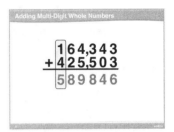

4.008 Subtracting Multi-Digit Whole Numbers (4.NBT.B.4)

Students apply a similar strategy as in the previous lesson to subtract six-digit numbers in columns. They start by subtracting the digits in the ones column and move left to the digits in the tens column, then to the hundreds, and so on. Problems progress from subtraction with no regrouping to subtraction with regrouping.

4.009 Multiplying Whole Numbers by a One-Digit Number (4.NBT.B.5)

Continuing the strategy of performing operations by place value, students learn how to multiply up to four-digit numbers by a one-digit number—both with and without regrouping.

4.010 Multiplying 2-Digit Numbers by 2-Digit Numbers (4.NBT.B.5)

To multiply two-digit numbers by two-digit numbers, students learn to decompose the numbers into smaller numbers that they can easily multiply. For example, to multiply 16 × 14, students decompose 16 to 10 + 6 and 14 to 10 + 4. They then multiply 10 × 10, 10 × 6, 10 × 4, and 6 × 4, then add their products. They also learn to apply partial products when multiplying the numbers in columns.

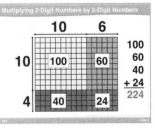

4.011 Equal Fractions (4.NF.A.1)

Given a fraction, students learn that they can find an equal fraction simply by multiplying both the numerator and denominator by the same number. For example, by multiplying both the numerator and denominator of 3/4 by 2, students find that 6/8 is equal to 3/4.

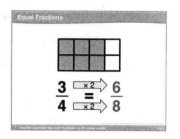

4.012 Comparing Fractions (4.NF.A.2)

This lesson demonstrates a shortcut for comparing fractions: Given two fractions, multiply the denominator of the second fraction with the numerator of the first fraction and write the product above the first fraction. Then multiply the denominator of the first fraction with the numerator of the second fraction and write the product above the second fraction. Finally, compare the first product to see if it's greater than, less than, or equal to the second product. If the first product is greater than the second product, then the first fraction is greater than the second fraction.

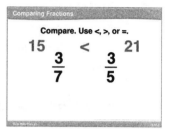

4.013 Comparing to Benchmark Fractions (4.NF.A.2)

In this lesson, students compare fractions to benchmark fractions 1/2 and 1/4. To compare a fraction, such as 43/80, to 1/2, students ask if the numerator *(43)* is half of the denominator *(80)*. In this particular example, since 43 is more than half of 80, it follows that the fraction is greater than 1/2. Students apply the same strategy to compare fractions with 1/4.

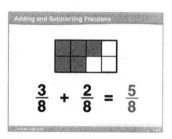

4.014 Adding and Subtracting Fractions (4.NF.B.3)

Students learn that when they add fractions with the same denominators (for example, 8ths), the sum will also have the same denominator, and they simply need to add the numerators (3/8 + 2/8 = 5/8). By the same token, when they subtract two fractions with the same denominators, the difference will also have the same denominator, and they simply have to subtract the numerators.

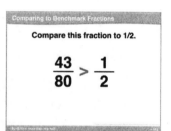

4.015 Mixed Numbers to Improper Fractions (4.NF.B.3)

Presented with a mixed number, such as $2\frac{1}{4}$, students learn two strategies for determining the improper fraction it is equivalent to. First is through a visual representation of the mixed number, in which they count how many parts there are in all *(9)*. In the second strategy, students multiply the denominator of the fraction with the whole number *(4 x 2)*, which shows how many fractional parts there are in the whole number. Then they add the numerator to find the total number of parts *(9/4)*.

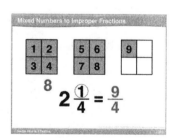

4.016 Understanding Fractions as Multiples of Unit Fractions (4.NF.B.4)

With the help of visuals, students see that a fraction, such as 3/4, is the sum of its unit fractions, such as 1/4 + 1/4 + 1/4. After a few more examples, students begin to see that since the unit fraction is added a number of times, they can simply multiply the unit fraction by the number of times it is added; for example, 3/4 = 3 × 1/4. Students then see that to get the product of a whole number and a fraction, they can multiply the whole number by the fraction's numerator and keep the denominator.

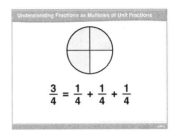

4.017 Multiplying Fractions by Whole Numbers (4.NF.B.4)

Students find what the fraction of a whole number is equivalent to with the help of more visuals. For example, to determine what 3/4 of 8 is, students are presented with 8 circles divided into 4 groups. Three of the groups are then colored, and they see that 3/4 of 8 is 6. A quicker strategy involves division and multiplication. The whole number *(8)* is divided by the denominator *(4)*, and the resulting quotient *(2)* is multiplied by the numerator *(3)*. The answer is still 6.

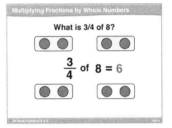

4.018 Adding Fractions With Denominators 10 and 100 (4.NF.C.5)

Students learn how to express a fraction with denominator 10 into a fraction with denominator 100—they simply multiply both the numerator and denominator by 10. Armed with this knowledge, students can then add two fractions with denominators 10 and 100 by first converting the fractions so they both have the same denominator, then adding their numerators.

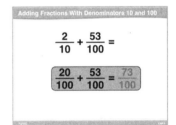

4.019 Reading Decimal Models (4.NF.C.6)

Students are introduced to decimals through fractions and models. They learn, for example, that 1/10 is equal to 0.1 and 1/100 is equal to 0.01. Given a square that has been divided into 100 smaller squares, students identify the decimal it represents by looking at how many small squares are colored.

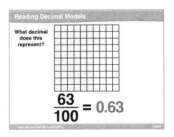

4.020 Comparing Decimals (4.NF.C.7)

After a brief review of comparing whole numbers, students move on to compare decimals. They learn that when comparing decimals, it is important to line up the decimal points to ensure that the places are aligned properly. Then they can compare the digits at each place, starting with the largest place.

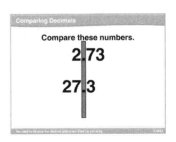

11

4.021 Finding the Area of a Rectangle (4.MD.A.3)

To find the area of a rectangle, students first divide it into square units then multiply the length by the width. Later, they use standard units of measurement to express the area of various rectangles.

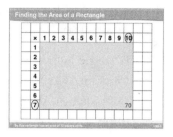

4.022 Angles, Circles, and Protractors (4.MD.C.5, 4.MD.C.6)

This lesson shows that when two rays share an endpoint, they form an angle. The measure of that angle describes part of a circle. A full circle is 360°. Students learn how to read and estimate the measure of various angles.

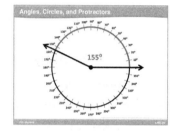

4.023 Sketching Angles (4.MD.C.6)

Using a protractor on the screen, students draw different angles and measure them. After learning how to estimate the measure of an angle, they also learn some strategies for drawing certain angles (such as 90°, 45°, 60°, and so on) without a protractor.

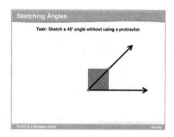

4.024 Parallel Lines and Parallelograms (4.G.A.1, 4.G.A.2)

Students identify *parallel lines* (lines in the same plane that never intersect) and *parallelograms*, which are quadrilaterals that have two sets of opposite sides that are parallel.

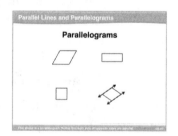

4.025 Line Symmetry (4.G.A.3)

Looking at some basic shapes, students notice that when a line of symmetry divides a shape in half, one side of the shape is a congruent reflection of the other side. Not all dividing lines are lines of symmetry. While a trapezoid has only one line of symmetry, other shapes can have more than one, while others have no symmetry at all. Students learn to draw a symmetrical figure by drawing a reflection of the figure on the other side of a line of symmetry.

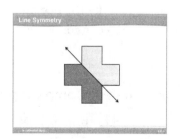

Meeting the Common Core State Standards

The lessons and activities in this resource meet the following Common Core State Standards for Mathematics. For more information, visit the CCSSI website at **www.corestandards.org/math**.

Operations and Algebraic Thinking (4.OA)

Use the four operations with whole numbers to solve problems.

4.OA.A.1 Interpret a multiplication equation as a comparison, e.g., interpret $35 = 5 \times 7$ as a statement that 35 is 5 times as many as 7 and 7 times as many as 5. Represent verbal statements of multiplicative comparisons as multiplication equations.

Gain familiarity with factors and multiples.

4.OA.B.4 Find all factor pairs for a whole number in the range 1–100. Recognize that a whole number is a multiple of each of its factors. Determine whether a given whole number in the range 1–100 is a multiple of a given one-digit number. Determine whether a given whole number in the range 1–100 is prime or composite.

Number & Operations in Base Ten (4.NBT)

Generalize place value understanding for multi-digit whole numbers.

4.NBT.A.1 Recognize that in a multi-digit whole number, a digit in one place represents ten times what it represents in the place to its right.

4.NBT.A.2 Read and write multi-digit whole numbers using base-ten numerals, number names, and expanded form. Compare two multi-digit numbers based on meanings of the digits in each place, using >, =, and < symbols to record the results of comparisons.

4.NBT.A.3 Use place value understanding to round multi-digit whole numbers to any place.

Use place value understanding and properties of operations to perform multi-digit arithmetic.

4.NBT.B.4 Fluently add and subtract multi-digit whole numbers using the standard algorithm.

4.NBT.B.5 Multiply a whole number of up to four digits by a one-digit whole number, and multiply two two-digit numbers, using strategies based on place value and the properties of operations. Illustrate and explain the calculation by using equations, rectangular arrays, and/or area models.

Number & Operations—Fractions (4.NF)

Extend understanding of fraction equivalence and ordering.

4.NF.A.1 Explain why a fraction a/b is equivalent to a fraction $(n \times a)/(n \times b)$ by using visual fraction models, with attention to how the number and size of the parts differ even though the two fractions themselves are the same size. Use this principle to recognize and generate equivalent fractions.

4.NF.A.2 Compare two fractions with different numerators and different denominators, e.g., by creating common denominators or numerators, or by comparing to a benchmark fraction such as 1/2. Recognize that comparisons are valid only when the two fractions refer to the same whole. Record the results of comparisons with symbols >, =, or <, and justify the conclusions, e.g., by using a visual fraction model.

Build fractions from unit fractions by applying and extending previous understandings of operations on whole numbers.

4.NF.B.3 Understand a fraction a/b with $a > 1$ as a sum of fractions $1/b$.

    4.NF.B.3a Understand addition and subtraction of fractions as joining and separating parts referring to the same whole.

    4.NF.B.3b Decompose a fraction into a sum of fractions with the same denominator in more than one way, recording each decomposition by an equation. Justify decompositions, e.g., by using a visual fraction model.

4.NF.B.4 Apply and extend previous understandings of multiplication to multiply a fraction by a whole number.

    4.NF.B.4a Understand a fraction a/b as a multiple of $1/b$.

    4.NF.B.4b Understand a multiple of a/b as a multiple of $1/b$, and use this understanding to multiply a fraction by a whole number.

Understand decimal notation for fractions, and compare decimal fractions

4.NF.C.5 Express a fraction with denominator 10 as an equivalent fraction with denominator 100, and use this technique to add two fractions with respective denominators 10 and 100.2.

4.NF.C.6 Use decimal notation for fractions with denominators 10 or 100.

4.NF.C.7 Compare two decimals to hundredths by reasoning about their size. Recognize that comparisons are valid only when the two decimals refer to the same whole. Record the results of comparisons with the symbols >, =, or <, and justify the conclusions, e.g., by using a visual model.

Measurement & Data (4.MD)

Solve problems involving measurement and conversion of measurements from a larger unit to a smaller unit.

4.MD.A.3 Apply the area and perimeter formulas for rectangles in real world and mathematical problems.

Geometric measurement: understand concepts of angle and measure angles.

4.MD.C.5 Recognize angles as geometric shapes that are formed wherever two rays share a common endpoint, and understand concepts of angle measurement:

> **4.MD.C.5a** An angle is measured with reference to a circle with its center at the common endpoint of the rays, by considering the fraction of the circular arc between the points where the two rays intersect the circle. An angle that turns through 1/360 of a circle is called a "one-degree angle," and can be used to measure angles.

> **4.MD.C.5b** An angle that turns through n one-degree angles is said to have an angle measure of n degrees.

4.MD.C.6 Measure angles in whole-number degrees using a protractor. Sketch angles of specified measure.

Geometry (4.G)

Draw and identify lines and angles, and classify shapes by properties of their lines and angles.

4.G.A.1 Draw points, lines, line segments, rays, angles (right, acute, obtuse), and perpendicular and parallel lines. Identify these in two-dimensional figures.

4.G.A.2 Classify two-dimensional figures based on the presence or absence of parallel or perpendicular lines, or the presence or absence of angles of a specified size. Recognize right triangles as a category, and identify right triangles.

4.G.A.3 Recognize a line of symmetry for a two-dimensional figure as a line across the figure such that the figure can be folded along the line into matching parts. Identify line-symmetric figures and draw lines of symmetry.

Understanding Multiplication: A

Name _____ Date _____

① Shade the multiples of 7 and the multiples of 8. What is the product of 7 and 8? _____

×	1	2	3	4	5	6	7	8	9	10
1	1	2	3	4	5	6	7	8	9	10
2	2	4	6	8	10	12	14	16	18	20
3	3	6	9	12	15	18	21	24	27	30
4	4	8	12	16	20	24	28	32	36	40
5	5	10	15	20	25	30	35	40	45	50
6	6	12	18	24	30	36	42	48	54	60
7	7	14	21	28	35	42	49	56	63	70
8	8	16	24	32	40	48	56	64	72	80
9	9	18	27	36	45	54	63	72	81	90
10	10	20	30	40	50	60	70	80	90	100

② Shade the multiples of 5 and the multiples of 8. What is the product of 5 and 8? _____

×	1	2	3	4	5	6	7	8	9	10
1	1	2	3	4	5	6	7	8	9	10
2	2	4	6	8	10	12	14	16	18	20
3	3	6	9	12	15	18	21	24	27	30
4	4	8	12	16	20	24	28	32	36	40
5	5	10	15	20	25	30	35	40	45	50
6	6	12	18	24	30	36	42	48	54	60
7	7	14	21	28	35	42	49	56	63	70
8	8	16	24	32	40	48	56	64	72	80
9	9	18	27	36	45	54	63	72	81	90
10	10	20	30	40	50	60	70	80	90	100

③ Shade the multiples of 3 and the multiples of 9. What is the product of 3 and 9? _____

×	1	2	3	4	5	6	7	8	9	10
1	1	2	3	4	5	6	7	8	9	10
2	2	4	6	8	10	12	14	16	18	20
3	3	6	9	12	15	18	21	24	27	30
4	4	8	12	16	20	24	28	32	36	40
5	5	10	15	20	25	30	35	40	45	50
6	6	12	18	24	30	36	42	48	54	60
7	7	14	21	28	35	42	49	56	63	70
8	8	16	24	32	40	48	56	64	72	80
9	9	18	27	36	45	54	63	72	81	90
10	10	20	30	40	50	60	70	80	90	100

④ Shade the multiples of 6 and the multiples of 7. What is the product of 6 and 7? _____

×	1	2	3	4	5	6	7	8	9	10
1	1	2	3	4	5	6	7	8	9	10
2	2	4	6	8	10	12	14	16	18	20
3	3	6	9	12	15	18	21	24	27	30
4	4	8	12	16	20	24	28	32	36	40
5	5	10	15	20	25	30	35	40	45	50
6	6	12	18	24	30	36	42	48	54	60
7	7	14	21	28	35	42	49	56	63	70
8	8	16	24	32	40	48	56	64	72	80
9	9	18	27	36	45	54	63	72	81	90
10	10	20	30	40	50	60	70	80	90	100

⑤ Shade the multiples of 4 and the multiples of 10. What is the product of 4 and 10? _____

×	1	2	3	4	5	6	7	8	9	10
1	1	2	3	4	5	6	7	8	9	10
2	2	4	6	8	10	12	14	16	18	20
3	3	6	9	12	15	18	21	24	27	30
4	4	8	12	16	20	24	28	32	36	40
5	5	10	15	20	25	30	35	40	45	50
6	6	12	18	24	30	36	42	48	54	60
7	7	14	21	28	35	42	49	56	63	70
8	8	16	24	32	40	48	56	64	72	80
9	9	18	27	36	45	54	63	72	81	90
10	10	20	30	40	50	60	70	80	90	100

⑥ Shade the multiples of 3 and the multiples of 5. What is the product of 3 and 5? _____

×	1	2	3	4	5	6	7	8	9	10
1	1	2	3	4	5	6	7	8	9	10
2	2	4	6	8	10	12	14	16	18	20
3	3	6	9	12	15	18	21	24	27	30
4	4	8	12	16	20	24	28	32	36	40
5	5	10	15	20	25	30	35	40	45	50
6	6	12	18	24	30	36	42	48	54	60
7	7	14	21	28	35	42	49	56	63	70
8	8	16	24	32	40	48	56	64	72	80
9	9	18	27	36	45	54	63	72	81	90
10	10	20	30	40	50	60	70	80	90	100

25 Common Core Math Lessons for the Interactive Whiteboard: Grade 4 © 2014 by Steve Wyborney, Scholastic Teaching Resources

Name _____ Date _____

① Show 3 sets of 5. (This one has been started for you.)

② Show 8 sets of 2.

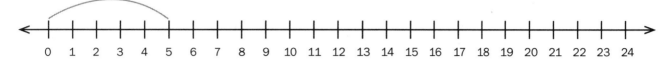

③ Show 5 sets of 4.

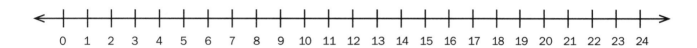

④ Show 4 sets of 6.

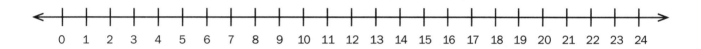

⑤ Show 3 sets of 8.

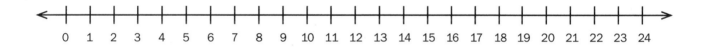

⑥ Show 7 sets of 3.

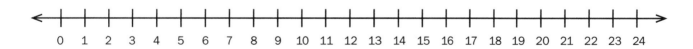

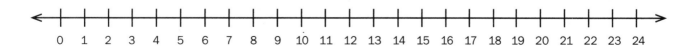

Name _____ Date _____

Write the product of each statement on the blank line below it.

① 5 sets of 3

_____

② 2 sets of 9

_____

③ 4 sets of 7

_____

④ 8 sets of 8

_____

⑤ 9 sets of 1

_____

⑥ 3 sets of 3

_____

⑦ 7 sets of 4

_____

⑧ 5 sets of 6

_____

⑨ 9 sets of 10

_____

⑩ 10 sets of 7

_____

⑪ 1 set of 3

_____

⑫ 8 sets of 4

_____

⑬ 7 sets of 8

_____

⑭ 8 sets of 6

_____

⑮ 6 sets of 9

_____

25 Common Core Math Lessons for the Interactive Whiteboard: Grade 4 © 2014 by Steve Wyborney, Scholastic Teaching Resources

Name _____ Date _____

Circle groups of 3. Is there a remainder? If so, shade the remainder.

① Is there a remainder? _____

○○○○○
○○○○○
○○○○○

② Is there a remainder? _____

□□□□
□□□□
□□□□
□□□□

③ Is there a remainder? _____

△△△△△△
△△△△△△

④ Is there a remainder? _____

○○○○○
○○○○○
○○○○○
○○○○○
○○○○○

⑤ Is there a remainder? _____

☆☆☆☆☆☆
☆☆☆☆☆☆
☆☆☆☆☆☆
☆☆☆☆☆☆

⑥ Is there a remainder? _____

◇◇◇◇◇◇◇
◇◇◇◇◇◇
◇◇◇◇◇◇◇

⑦ Is there a remainder? _____

□□□□□□□□□
□□□□□□□□
□□□□□□□□
□□□□□□□□□

⑧ Is there a remainder? _____

△△△△△△△
△△△△△△△
△△△△△△△
△△△△△△△
△△△△△△△

Name _____ Date _____

Find the sum of the digits. Is the number divisible by 3?

① **52**
What is the sum of the digits? _____
Is 52 divisible by 3? _____

② **555**
What is the sum of the digits? _____
Is 555 divisible by 3? _____

③ **911**
What is the sum of the digits? _____
Is 911 divisible by 3? _____

④ **531**
What is the sum of the digits? _____
Is 531 divisible by 3? _____

⑤ **746**
What is the sum of the digits? _____
Is 746 divisible by 3? _____

⑥ **834**
What is the sum of the digits? _____
Is 834 divisible by 3? _____

⑦ **384**
What is the sum of the digits? _____
Is 384 divisible by 3? _____

⑧ **795**
What is the sum of the digits? _____
Is 795 divisible by 3? _____

25 Common Core Math Lessons for the Interactive Whiteboard: Grade 4 © 2014 by Steve Wyborney, Scholastic Teaching Resources

Name _____ Date _____

Determine whether each number is divisible by 3. Write "YES" or "NO" below each number.

① 584   ② 326   ③ 738

_____   _____   _____

④ 514   ⑤ 2,061   ⑥ 7,261

_____   _____   _____

⑦ 58   ⑧ 756   ⑨ 218

_____   _____   _____

⑩ 474   ⑪ 8,026   ⑫ 3,936

_____   _____   _____

⑬ 78   ⑭ 485   ⑮ 655

_____   _____   _____

Name _____ Date _____

Find the factor pairs of the following numbers. Write them below each number.

①   6

_____

②   8

_____

③   9

_____

④   10

_____

⑤   12

_____

⑥   14

_____

⑦   15

_____

⑧   16

_____

25 Common Core Math Lessons for the Interactive Whiteboard: Grade 4 © 2014 by Steve Wyborney, Scholastic Teaching Resources

Name _____ Date _____

Find the factor pairs of the following numbers. Write them below each number.

①   **18**
_____

②   **20**
_____

③   **21**
_____

④   **24**
_____

⑤   **27**
_____

⑥   **30**
_____

⑦   **33**
_____

⑧   **36**
_____

Name _____ Date _____

Read each statement. Determine if it is true or false. Write T or F on the blank line.

_____ ① One of the factors of 18 is 6.

_____ ② 4 is a factor of 12.

_____ ③ The number 8 has 6 factors.

_____ ④ One of the factors of 16 is 4.

_____ ⑤ 14 is a factor of 21.

_____ ⑥ The number 15 has 4 factors.

_____ ⑦ One of the factors of 24 is 12.

_____ ⑧ 9 is a factor of 27.

_____ ⑨ The number 21 has 6 factors.

_____ ⑩ One of the factors of 24 is 9.

_____ ⑪ 8 is a factor of 15.

_____ ⑫ The number 24 has 8 factors.

25 Common Core Math Lessons for the Interactive Whiteboard: Grade 4 © 2014 By Steve Wyborney, Scholastic Teaching Resources

Name _____ Date _____

Write the value of the circled digit below each number. The first one has been done for you.

① 386,7̲28

_700_

② 2̲54,096

_____

③ 9̲13,060

_____

④ 752,87̲6

_____

⑤ 3̲0,695

_____

⑥ 4̲38,576

_____

⑦ 209,7̲60

_____

⑧ 831̲,796

_____

⑨ 2̲58,174

_____

⑩ 9̲45,337

_____

⑪ 125,6̲73

_____

⑫ 104,6̲48

_____

Name _____ Date _____

Write each number using expanded notation. The first one has been done for you.

① 495

400 + 90 + 5

② 3,916

③ 7,538

④ 637

⑤ 23,816

⑥ 70,481

⑦ 84,300

⑧ 738,264

⑨ 519,306

⑩ 463,745

25 Common Core Math Lessons for the Interactive Whiteboard: Grade 4 © 2014 by Steve Wyborney, Scholastic Teaching Resources

Name _____ Date _____

Write each number using standard form.

① 300 + 70 + 8

_____

② 2,000 + 300 + 50 + 2

_____

③ 50,000 + 6,000 + 400 + 90 + 2

_____

④ 300,000 + 7,000 + 60 + 4

_____

⑤ 60,000 + 7,000 + 5

_____

⑥ 5,000 + 500 + 30 + 6

_____

⑦ 200,000 + 30,000 + 90 + 8

_____

⑧ 900,000 + 10,000 + 2,000 + 500 + 40 + 3

_____

⑨ 80,000 + 5,000 + 200 + 30 + 9

_____

⑩ 50,000 + 3,000 + 600 + 90 + 4

_____

Name _____ Date _____

Compare. Use <, >, or =.

① 45 _____ 67

② 23 _____ 23

③ 16 _____ 19

④ 68 _____ 67

⑤ 59 _____ 59

⑥ 63 _____ 59

⑦ 284 _____ 248

⑧ 302 _____ 297

⑨ 613 _____ 613

⑩ 816 _____ 861

⑪ 340 _____ 304

⑫ 627 _____ 672

⑬ 1,216 _____ 1,612

⑭ 4,908 _____ 4,977

⑮ 6,991 _____ 6,990

Name _____ Date _____

Circle the place that determines which number is greater. Then compare. Use <, >, or =.

①   4,386

      4,335

4,386 _____ 4,335

②   2,357

      2,354

2,357 _____ 2,354

③   1,016

      2,569

1,016 _____ 2,569

④   17,324

      17,289

17,324 _____ 17,289

⑤   3,062

      2,552

3,062 _____ 2,552

⑥   63,812

      70,035

63,812 _____ 70,035

⑦   596,217

      583,412

596,217 _____ 583,412

⑧   154,316

      154,308

154,316 _____ 154,308

⑨   231,566

      238,492

231,566 _____ 238,492

Name _____ Date _____

Compare. Use <, >, or =.

① 23,524 _____ 23,518

② 68,254 _____ 61,933

③ 548,296 _____ 548,296

④ 313,056 _____ 700,038

⑤ 25,882 _____ 124,210

⑥ 6,058 _____ 14,254

⑦ 335,513 _____ 335,508

⑧ 621,214 _____ 612,215

⑨ 882,053 _____ 882,053

⑩ 796,267 _____ 769,267

25 Common Core Math Lessons for the Interactive Whiteboard: Grade 4 © 2014 by Steve Wyborney, Scholastic Teaching Resources

Name _____ Date _____

Circle the digit in the tens place.

① 16,284   ② 612   ③ 5,382

Circle the digit in the hundreds place.

④ 45,682   ⑤ 7,045   ⑥ 145,392

Circle the digit in the thousands place.

⑦ 684,329   ⑧ 54,692   ⑨ 703,926

Circle the digit in the ten-thousands place.

⑩ 405,273   ⑪ 695,273   ⑫ 53,612

Circle the digit in the hundred-thousands place.

⑬ 5,738,214   ⑭ 538,907   ⑮ 12,583,049

Name _____ Date _____

Underline the digit in the indicated place. Then draw a box around that digit and all the digits to the left to answer the question.

How many tens are there?

① 346 _____   ② 2,316 _____   ③ 17,309 _____

How many hundreds are there?

④ 3,614 _____   ⑤ 13,564 _____   ⑥ 293,587 _____

How many thousands are there?

⑦ 5,286 _____   ⑧ 69,208 _____   ⑨ 108,236 _____

How many ten-thousands are there?

⑩ 56,214 _____   ⑪ 785,403 _____   ⑫ 6,982,304 _____

How many hundred-thousands are there?

⑬ 486,295 _____   ⑭ 2,386,094 _____   ⑮ 382,561 _____

Name _____ Date _____

Round each number to the given place.

Round to the nearest ten.

① 523   ② 6,285   ③ 15,287

_____   _____   _____

Round to the nearest hundred.

④ 588   ⑤ 251,380   ⑥ 16,642

_____   _____   _____

Round to the nearest thousand.

⑦ 8,612   ⑧ 542,355   ⑨ 24,735

_____   _____   _____

Round to the nearest ten-thousand.

⑩ 62,308   ⑪ 159,062   ⑫ 74,287

_____   _____   _____

Round to the nearest hundred-thousand.

⑬ 556,731   ⑭ 6,315,296   ⑮ 672,208

_____   _____   _____

**Adding Multi-Digit
Whole Numbers: A**

Name _____ Date _____

This page features addition with no regrouping. Add and write the sum.

① 3,286
+ 1,501
_____

② 1,032
+ 4,835
_____

③ 5,264
+ 3,125
_____

④ 2,534
+ 4,325
_____

⑤ 3,295
+ 6,503
_____

⑥ 7,134
+ 1,362
_____

⑦ 51,163
+ 7,235
_____

⑧ 384
+ 24,311
_____

⑨ 54,021
+ 13,452
_____

⑩ 16,418
+ 23,511
_____

⑪ 44,902
+ 51,053
_____

⑫ 71,332
+ 15,365
_____

⑬ 463,012
+ 234,953
_____

⑭ 275,051
+ 520,635
_____

⑮ 702,633
+ 183,324
_____

34

Name _____ Date _____

This page features addition with some regrouping. Add and write the sum.

①   2,914
    + 3,821
    ⎯⎯⎯⎯

②   5,230
    + 3,582
    ⎯⎯⎯⎯

③   6,217
    + 5,822
    ⎯⎯⎯⎯

④   3,054
    + 2,138
    ⎯⎯⎯⎯

⑤   6,295
    + 7,374
    ⎯⎯⎯⎯

⑥   4,030
    + 3,582
    ⎯⎯⎯⎯

⑦   38,117
    + 54,235
    ⎯⎯⎯⎯

⑧   61,742
    + 35,872
    ⎯⎯⎯⎯

⑨   59,284
    + 31,396
    ⎯⎯⎯⎯

⑩   52,391
    + 48,227
    ⎯⎯⎯⎯

⑪   72,395
    + 86,208
    ⎯⎯⎯⎯

⑫   61,332
    + 74,028
    ⎯⎯⎯⎯

⑬   531,016
    + 182,937
    ⎯⎯⎯⎯

⑭   112,948
    + 639,125
    ⎯⎯⎯⎯

⑮   414,293
    + 183,324
    ⎯⎯⎯⎯

Name _____ Date _____

Add and write the sum.

①   5,234
   + 6,083
   ————

②   1,275
   + 4,302
   ————

③   5,974
   + 6,853
   ————

④   4,337
   + 6,088
   ————

⑤   1,004
   + 6,239
   ————

⑥   3,309
   + 7,788
   ————

⑦   43,228
   + 16,909
   ————

⑧   42,227
   + 34,767
   ————

⑨   35,229
   + 48,792
   ————

⑩   45,836
   + 55,821
   ————

⑪   44,534
   + 16,746
   ————

⑫   92,837
   + 54,231
   ————

⑬   631,297
   + 546,089
   ————

⑭   472,341
   + 572,146
   ————

⑮   346,260
   + 924,598
   ————

Name _____ Date _____

This page features subtraction with no regrouping. Subtract and write the difference.

① 287
  − 132
  ——

② 956
  − 224
  ——

③ 717
  − 214
  ——

④ 3,564
  − 3,250
  ——

⑤ 7,894
  − 3,103
  ——

⑥ 6,183
  − 5,122
  ——

⑦ 4,956
  − 1,953
  ——

⑧ 3,047
  − 3,031
  ——

⑨ 7,384
  − 5,384
  ——

⑩ 24,295
  − 13,233
  ——

⑪ 87,614
  − 30,213
  ——

⑫ 53,299
  − 21,235
  ——

⑬ 748,299
  − 312,259
  ——

⑭ 374,546
  − 354,416
  ——

⑮ 296,417
  − 162,416
  ——

Name _____ Date _____

This page features subtraction with some regrouping. Subtract and write the difference.

①
$$532$$
$$- 216$$
———

②
$$872$$
$$- 191$$
———

③
$$345$$
$$- 138$$
———

④
$$524$$
$$- 287$$
———

⑤
$$618$$
$$- 258$$
———

⑥
$$765$$
$$- 216$$
———

⑦
$$3,414$$
$$- 2,086$$
———

⑧
$$7,329$$
$$- 2,884$$
———

⑨
$$8,634$$
$$- 2,070$$
———

⑩
$$2,526$$
$$- 2,509$$
———

⑪
$$7,354$$
$$- 2,061$$
———

⑫
$$3,835$$
$$- 2,698$$
———

⑬
$$64,702$$
$$- 51,900$$
———

⑭
$$87,131$$
$$- 62,826$$
———

⑮
$$31,552$$
$$- 28,298$$
———

25 Common Core Math Lessons for the Interactive Whiteboard: Grade 4 © 2014 by Steve Wyborney, Scholastic Teaching Resources

Name _____ Date _____

Subtract and write the difference.

①   538
     – 201
     ———

②   795
     – 288
     ———

③   694
     – 517
     ———

④   325
     – 198
     ———

⑤   634
     – 591
     ———

⑥   715
     – 689
     ———

⑦   2,516
     – 1,516
     ———

⑧   3,209
     – 2,704
     ———

⑨   3,841
     – 2,817
     ———

⑩   3,978
     – 2,879
     ———

⑪   5,216
     – 3,017
     ———

⑫   8,524
     – 2,518
     ———

⑬   23,619
     – 20,882
     ———

⑭   15,281
     – 13,685
     ———

⑮   54,991
     – 37,258
     ———

Name _____ Date _____

This page features multiplication with no regrouping. Multiply and write the product.

①
```
    23
x    2
_____
```

②
```
    15
x    1
_____
```

③
```
    12
x    4
_____
```

④
```
    57
x    1
_____
```

⑤
```
    40
x    2
_____
```

⑥
```
    71
x    5
_____
```

⑦
```
    32
x    3
_____
```

⑧
```
    83
x    3
_____
```

⑨
```
    61
x    6
_____
```

⑩
```
   134
x    2
_____
```

⑪
```
   522
x    4
_____
```

⑫
```
   703
x    3
_____
```

⑬
```
   487
x    1
_____
```

⑭
```
   834
x    2
_____
```

⑮
```
   201
x    5
_____
```

Name _____ Date _____

This page features multiplication with some regrouping. Multiply and write the product.

①   23
    x   4
    _____

②   62
    x   5
    _____

③   73
    x   7
    _____

④   65
    x   4
    _____

⑤   86
    x   5
    _____

⑥   39
    x   3
    _____

⑦   216
    x   4
    _____

⑧   538
    x   7
    _____

⑨   624
    x   3
    _____

⑩   874
    x   9
    _____

⑪   732
    x   7
    _____

⑫   824
    x   8
    _____

⑬   903
    x   5
    _____

⑭   711
    x   8
    _____

⑮   598
    x   9
    _____

Name _____ Date _____

Multiply and write the product.

①
```
    64
×    5
_____
```

②
```
    73
×    6
_____
```

③
```
    85
×    9
_____
```

④
```
   682
×    4
_____
```

⑤
```
   395
×    1
_____
```

⑥
```
   817
×    7
_____
```

⑦
```
   562
×    5
_____
```

⑧
```
   254
×    8
_____
```

⑨
```
   682
×    3
_____
```

⑩
```
  1,586
×     4
_____
```

⑪
```
  3,916
×     8
_____
```

⑫
```
  2,017
×     6
_____
```

⑬
```
  7,586
×     2
_____
```

⑭
```
  8,084
×     7
_____
```

⑮
```
  5,964
×     8
_____
```

25 Common Core Math Lessons for the Interactive Whiteboard: Grade 4 © 2014 by Steve Wyborney, Scholastic Teaching Resources

Name _____ Date _____

Find each partial product. Write the products inside the correct rectangle. Then add the four products together. Use the answer to complete the equation.

① | 14 x 17 =

x	10	7
10		
4		

② | 13 x 19 =

x	10	9
10		
3		

③ | 18 x 13 =

x	10	3
10		
8		

④ | 15 x 15 =

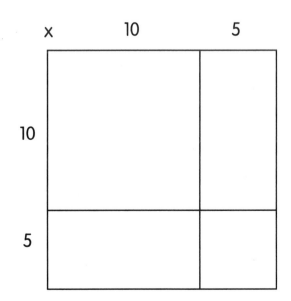

x	10	5
10		
5		

25 Common Core Math Lessons for the Interactive Whiteboard: Grade 4 © 2014 by Steve Wyborney, Scholastic Teaching Resources

Name _____ Date _____

This page features multiplication with some regrouping. Multiply and write the product.

①   52
    × 13
    _____

②   61
    × 42
    _____

③   73
    × 81
    _____

④   71
    × 64
    _____

⑤   94
    × 21
    _____

⑥   52
    × 63
    _____

⑦   83
    × 63
    _____

⑧   52
    × 71
    _____

⑨   64
    × 22
    _____

Name _____ Date _____

Multiply and write the product.

①   35
    x   64
    _____

②   83
    x   29
    _____

③   78
    x   53
    _____

④   29
    x   47
    _____

⑤   62
    x   18
    _____

⑥   31
    x   57
    _____

⑦   59
    x   47
    _____

⑧   73
    x   28
    _____

⑨   86
    x   94
    _____

25 Common Core Math Lessons for the Interactive Whiteboard: Grade 4 © 2014 by Steve Wyborney, Scholastic Teaching Resources

Name _____ Date _____

Complete each expression by writing a function, such as _x 3_ or _÷ 6_, inside each arrow.

① 3 ➤ 15

② 4 ➤ 32

③ 8 ➤ 24

④ 27 ➤ 9

⑤ 7 ➤ 56

⑥ 35 ➤ 5

⑦ 7 ➤ 21

⑧ 42 ➤ 6

⑨ 54 ➤ 6

⑩ 5 ➤ 40

⑪ 48 ➤ 8

⑫ 8 ➤ 16

⑬ 50 ➤ 5

⑭ 6 ➤ 18

⑮ 54 ➤ 6

25 Common Core Math Lessons for the Interactive Whiteboard: Grade 4 © 2014 by Steve Wyborney, Scholastic Teaching Resources

Name _____ Date _____

Write the missing numerator or the missing denominator.

① $\dfrac{2}{3} = \dfrac{}{12}$

② $\dfrac{3}{5} = \dfrac{}{30}$

③ $\dfrac{4}{7} = \dfrac{}{35}$

④ $\dfrac{4}{6} = \dfrac{12}{}$

⑤ $\dfrac{5}{9} = \dfrac{40}{}$

⑥ $\dfrac{1}{3} = \dfrac{7}{}$

⑦ $\dfrac{21}{35} = \dfrac{3}{}$

⑧ $\dfrac{18}{63} = \dfrac{2}{}$

⑨ $\dfrac{18}{30} = \dfrac{3}{}$

⑩ $\dfrac{15}{25} = \dfrac{}{5}$

⑪ $\dfrac{50}{70} = \dfrac{}{7}$

⑫ $\dfrac{18}{30} = \dfrac{}{5}$

⑬ $\dfrac{6}{7} = \dfrac{}{42}$

⑭ $\dfrac{4}{5} = \dfrac{}{45}$

⑮ $\dfrac{1}{3} = \dfrac{}{15}$

Name _____ Date _____

Write the missing numerator or the missing denominator.

① $\dfrac{}{2} = \dfrac{6}{12}$

② $\dfrac{3}{4} = \dfrac{15}{}$

③ $\dfrac{6}{9} = \dfrac{42}{}$

④ $\dfrac{3}{4} = \dfrac{}{12}$

⑤ $\dfrac{2}{} = \dfrac{4}{20}$

⑥ $\dfrac{}{7} = \dfrac{48}{56}$

⑦ $\dfrac{32}{} = \dfrac{4}{7}$

⑧ $\dfrac{}{3} = \dfrac{14}{21}$

⑨ $\dfrac{1}{5} = \dfrac{}{40}$

⑩ $\dfrac{3}{9} = \dfrac{27}{}$

⑪ $\dfrac{}{5} = \dfrac{24}{30}$

⑫ $\dfrac{7}{8} = \dfrac{}{16}$

⑬ $\dfrac{3}{5} = \dfrac{15}{}$

⑭ $\dfrac{4}{} = \dfrac{28}{49}$

⑮ $\dfrac{}{40} = \dfrac{2}{5}$

25 Common Core Math Lessons for the Interactive Whiteboard: Grade 4 © 2014 by Steve Wyborney, Scholastic Teaching Resources

Name _____ Date _____

Compare each pair of fractions. Use <, >, or =.

① $\dfrac{1}{3}$ $\dfrac{3}{4}$

② $\dfrac{2}{5}$ $\dfrac{2}{3}$

③ $\dfrac{1}{8}$ $\dfrac{1}{5}$

④ $\dfrac{3}{4}$ $\dfrac{5}{7}$

⑤ $\dfrac{2}{9}$ $\dfrac{3}{10}$

⑥ $\dfrac{4}{5}$ $\dfrac{7}{9}$

⑦ $\dfrac{3}{4}$ $\dfrac{6}{8}$

⑧ $\dfrac{1}{2}$ $\dfrac{4}{7}$

⑨ $\dfrac{3}{5}$ $\dfrac{6}{10}$

⑩ $\dfrac{2}{9}$ $\dfrac{1}{5}$

⑪ $\dfrac{3}{4}$ $\dfrac{2}{3}$

⑫ $\dfrac{5}{7}$ $\dfrac{6}{9}$

⑬ $\dfrac{1}{2}$ $\dfrac{1}{5}$

⑭ $\dfrac{3}{4}$ $\dfrac{4}{5}$

⑮ $\dfrac{2}{9}$ $\dfrac{3}{7}$

Name _____ Date _____

Compare each pair of fractions. Use <, >, or =.

① $\dfrac{2}{3}$ $\dfrac{6}{8}$

② $\dfrac{1}{5}$ $\dfrac{2}{9}$

③ $\dfrac{3}{8}$ $\dfrac{2}{5}$

④ $\dfrac{2}{4}$ $\dfrac{5}{10}$

⑤ $\dfrac{2}{3}$ $\dfrac{6}{10}$

⑥ $\dfrac{2}{5}$ $\dfrac{7}{8}$

⑦ $\dfrac{1}{4}$ $\dfrac{2}{8}$

⑧ $\dfrac{1}{2}$ $\dfrac{3}{7}$

⑨ $\dfrac{2}{5}$ $\dfrac{4}{9}$

⑩ $\dfrac{3}{9}$ $\dfrac{1}{3}$

⑪ $\dfrac{4}{7}$ $\dfrac{2}{3}$

⑫ $\dfrac{5}{6}$ $\dfrac{6}{7}$

⑬ $\dfrac{1}{8}$ $\dfrac{2}{3}$

⑭ $\dfrac{3}{4}$ $\dfrac{1}{10}$

⑮ $\dfrac{3}{8}$ $\dfrac{4}{10}$

25 Common Core Math Lessons for the Interactive Whiteboard: Grade 4 © 2014 by Steve Wyborney, Scholastic Teaching Resources

Name _____ Date _____

Compare each pair of fractions. Use <, >, or =.

① $\dfrac{3}{5}$ $\dfrac{2}{3}$

② $\dfrac{1}{4}$ $\dfrac{2}{8}$

③ $\dfrac{4}{5}$ $\dfrac{8}{10}$

④ $\dfrac{1}{5}$ $\dfrac{2}{9}$

⑤ $\dfrac{4}{8}$ $\dfrac{5}{10}$

⑥ $\dfrac{6}{7}$ $\dfrac{7}{8}$

⑦ $\dfrac{3}{4}$ $\dfrac{7}{8}$

⑧ $\dfrac{2}{2}$ $\dfrac{8}{8}$

⑨ $\dfrac{2}{8}$ $\dfrac{3}{9}$

⑩ $\dfrac{7}{9}$ $\dfrac{2}{3}$

⑪ $\dfrac{3}{7}$ $\dfrac{2}{5}$

⑫ $\dfrac{3}{4}$ $\dfrac{7}{10}$

⑬ $\dfrac{5}{8}$ $\dfrac{2}{3}$

⑭ $\dfrac{4}{7}$ $\dfrac{8}{9}$

⑮ $\dfrac{4}{5}$ $\dfrac{3}{4}$

Name _____ Date _____

Compare each fraction to the benchmark fraction ½. Use <, >, or =.

①
$$\frac{24}{50} \qquad \frac{1}{2}$$

②
$$\frac{49}{100} \qquad \frac{1}{2}$$

③
$$\frac{99}{200} \qquad \frac{1}{2}$$

④
$$\frac{38}{50} \qquad \frac{1}{2}$$

⑤
$$\frac{41}{100} \qquad \frac{1}{2}$$

⑥
$$\frac{23}{40} \qquad \frac{1}{2}$$

⑦
$$\frac{17}{30} \qquad \frac{1}{2}$$

⑧
$$\frac{59}{100} \qquad \frac{1}{2}$$

⑨
$$\frac{104}{200} \qquad \frac{1}{2}$$

⑩
$$\frac{52}{100} \qquad \frac{1}{2}$$

⑪
$$\frac{23}{50} \qquad \frac{1}{2}$$

⑫
$$\frac{28}{50} \qquad \frac{1}{2}$$

Name _____ Date _____

Compare each fraction to the benchmark fraction ¼. Use <, >, or =.

① $\dfrac{9}{40}$ $\dfrac{1}{4}$

② $\dfrac{26}{100}$ $\dfrac{1}{4}$

③ $\dfrac{25}{100}$ $\dfrac{1}{4}$

④ $\dfrac{19}{80}$ $\dfrac{1}{4}$

⑤ $\dfrac{23}{80}$ $\dfrac{1}{4}$

⑥ $\dfrac{20}{80}$ $\dfrac{1}{4}$

⑦ $\dfrac{16}{100}$ $\dfrac{1}{4}$

⑧ $\dfrac{22}{100}$ $\dfrac{1}{4}$

⑨ $\dfrac{4}{20}$ $\dfrac{1}{4}$

⑩ $\dfrac{100}{400}$ $\dfrac{1}{4}$

⑪ $\dfrac{103}{400}$ $\dfrac{1}{4}$

⑫ $\dfrac{98}{400}$ $\dfrac{1}{4}$

Name _____ Date _____

Compare each fraction to the benchmark fraction $\frac{1}{5}$. Use <, >, or =.

① $\dfrac{10}{50}$ $\dfrac{1}{5}$

② $\dfrac{9}{50}$ $\dfrac{1}{5}$

③ $\dfrac{13}{50}$ $\dfrac{1}{5}$

④ $\dfrac{19}{100}$ $\dfrac{1}{5}$

⑤ $\dfrac{20}{100}$ $\dfrac{1}{5}$

⑥ $\dfrac{22}{100}$ $\dfrac{1}{5}$

⑦ $\dfrac{2}{10}$ $\dfrac{1}{5}$

⑧ $\dfrac{3}{10}$ $\dfrac{1}{5}$

⑨ $\dfrac{1}{10}$ $\dfrac{1}{5}$

⑩ $\dfrac{7}{50}$ $\dfrac{1}{5}$

⑪ $\dfrac{11}{50}$ $\dfrac{1}{5}$

⑫ $\dfrac{8}{50}$ $\dfrac{1}{5}$

Name _____ Date _____

Add the fractions and write the sum.

① $\dfrac{1}{5} + \dfrac{2}{5} =$

② $\dfrac{3}{8} + \dfrac{4}{8} =$

③ $\dfrac{1}{10} + \dfrac{3}{10} =$

④ $\dfrac{4}{5} + \dfrac{1}{5} =$

⑤ $\dfrac{1}{3} + \dfrac{2}{3} =$

⑥ $\dfrac{1}{4} + \dfrac{1}{4} =$

⑦ $\dfrac{3}{8} + \dfrac{4}{8} =$

⑧ $\dfrac{1}{10} + \dfrac{3}{10} =$

⑨ $\dfrac{4}{8} + \dfrac{1}{8} =$

⑩ $\dfrac{3}{7} + \dfrac{3}{7} =$

⑪ $\dfrac{3}{4} + \dfrac{0}{4} =$

⑫ $\dfrac{5}{9} + \dfrac{2}{9} =$

⑬ $\dfrac{1}{8} + \dfrac{8}{8} =$

⑭ $\dfrac{2}{3} + \dfrac{2}{3} =$

⑮ $\dfrac{3}{9} + \dfrac{2}{9} =$

Name _____ Date _____

Subtract the fractions and write the difference.

①
$$\frac{4}{10} - \frac{2}{10} =$$

②
$$\frac{7}{8} - \frac{3}{8} =$$

③
$$\frac{5}{6} - \frac{3}{6} =$$

④
$$\frac{2}{3} - \frac{2}{3} =$$

⑤
$$\frac{7}{4} - \frac{5}{4} =$$

⑥
$$\frac{3}{4} - \frac{1}{4} =$$

⑦
$$\frac{6}{8} - \frac{1}{8} =$$

⑧
$$\frac{9}{10} - \frac{7}{10} =$$

⑨
$$\frac{5}{8} - \frac{0}{8} =$$

⑩
$$\frac{6}{7} - \frac{2}{7} =$$

⑪
$$\frac{5}{4} - \frac{3}{4} =$$

⑫
$$\frac{10}{9} - \frac{7}{9} =$$

⑬
$$\frac{5}{8} - \frac{1}{8} =$$

⑭
$$\frac{3}{3} - \frac{2}{3} =$$

⑮
$$\frac{8}{9} - \frac{1}{9} =$$

Name _____ Date _____

Add or subtract the fractions and write the answer.

① $\dfrac{3}{4} - \dfrac{2}{4} =$

② $\dfrac{3}{10} + \dfrac{5}{10} =$

③ $\dfrac{4}{9} - \dfrac{3}{9} =$

④ $\dfrac{5}{8} + \dfrac{5}{8} =$

⑤ $\dfrac{3}{5} + \dfrac{1}{5} =$

⑥ $\dfrac{2}{4} - \dfrac{1}{4} =$

⑦ $\dfrac{7}{8} - \dfrac{5}{8} =$

⑧ $\dfrac{4}{9} - \dfrac{1}{9} =$

⑨ $\dfrac{7}{10} + \dfrac{2}{10} =$

⑩ $\dfrac{5}{8} - \dfrac{2}{8} =$

⑪ $\dfrac{6}{8} + \dfrac{1}{8} =$

⑫ $\dfrac{3}{10} - \dfrac{1}{10} =$

⑬ $\dfrac{2}{7} + \dfrac{1}{7} =$

⑭ $\dfrac{4}{5} - \dfrac{1}{5} =$

⑮ $\dfrac{2}{3} + \dfrac{1}{3} =$

Name _____ Date _____

What mixed number is shown?

①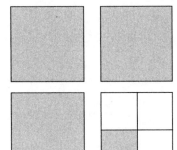

②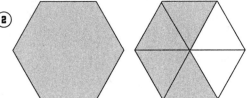

_____   _____

③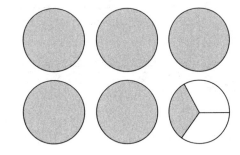

④

_____   _____

⑤

⑥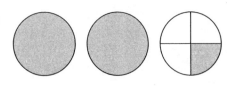

_____   _____

58

Name _____ Date _____

Convert each mixed number to an improper fraction.

① $8 \dfrac{2}{4} =$

② $3 \dfrac{1}{2} =$

③ $2 \dfrac{5}{8} =$

④ $1 \dfrac{1}{10} =$

⑤ $4 \dfrac{3}{5} =$

⑥ $5 \dfrac{2}{7} =$

⑦ $5 \dfrac{1}{2} =$

⑧ $2 \dfrac{5}{6} =$

⑨ $3 \dfrac{1}{8} =$

⑩ $4 \dfrac{2}{3} =$

⑪ $3 \dfrac{4}{5} =$

⑫ $4 \dfrac{1}{6} =$

⑬ $2 \dfrac{7}{10} =$

⑭ $3 \dfrac{2}{9} =$

⑮ $5 \dfrac{3}{5} =$

Name _____ Date _____

Convert each mixed number to an improper fraction.

① $3 \dfrac{3}{4} =$

② $5 \dfrac{1}{10} =$

③ $2 \dfrac{1}{5} =$

④ $4 \dfrac{3}{4} =$

⑤ $6 \dfrac{1}{5} =$

⑥ $8 \dfrac{1}{2} =$

⑦ $7 \dfrac{2}{3} =$

⑧ $1 \dfrac{3}{5} =$

⑨ $2 \dfrac{7}{8} =$

⑩ $4 \dfrac{1}{5} =$

⑪ $2 \dfrac{3}{4} =$

⑫ $6 \dfrac{7}{10} =$

⑬ $1 \dfrac{4}{5} =$

⑭ $3 \dfrac{1}{4} =$

⑮ $7 \dfrac{3}{8} =$

Name _____ Date _____

Write the fraction of the shape that is shaded. Then write an equivalent expression using unit fractions. The first one has been done for you.

①

$$\frac{3}{4} = \frac{1}{4} + \frac{1}{4} + \frac{1}{4}$$

②

_____

③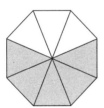

④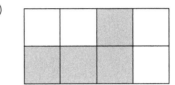

_____

_____

⑤

⑥

_____

_____

⑦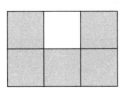

⑧

_____

_____

Name _____ Date _____

Write an equivalent expression using unit fractions. The first one has been done for you.

① $\dfrac{4}{5} = \dfrac{1}{5} + \dfrac{1}{5} + \dfrac{1}{5} + \dfrac{1}{5}$

_____

② $\dfrac{3}{7} =$

_____

③ $\dfrac{2}{3} =$

_____

④ $\dfrac{5}{8} =$

_____

⑤ $\dfrac{3}{4} =$

_____

⑥ $\dfrac{5}{5} =$

_____

⑦ $\dfrac{3}{8} =$

_____

⑧ $\dfrac{2}{4} =$

_____

⑨ $\dfrac{4}{10} =$

_____

⑩ $\dfrac{3}{5} =$

_____

⑪ $\dfrac{5}{9} =$

_____

⑫ $\dfrac{4}{4} =$

_____

⑬ $\dfrac{2}{6} =$

_____

⑭ $\dfrac{4}{7} =$

_____

Name _____ Date _____

Complete each equation. The first one has been done for you.

① $3 \times \dfrac{1}{4} = \dfrac{3}{4}$

② $3 \times \dfrac{1}{8} = $ _____

③ $7 \times \dfrac{1}{10} = $ _____

④ _____ $\times \dfrac{1}{5} = \dfrac{2}{5}$

⑤ $6 \times $ _____ $= \dfrac{6}{8}$

⑥ $5 \times \dfrac{1}{9} = $ _____

⑦ $9 \times \dfrac{1}{10} = $ _____

⑧ $3 \times \dfrac{1}{5} = $ _____

⑨ _____ $\times \dfrac{1}{10} = \dfrac{6}{10}$

⑩ $5 \times $ _____ $= \dfrac{5}{7}$

⑪ $5 \times \dfrac{1}{6} = $ _____

⑫ $7 \times $ _____ $= \dfrac{7}{8}$

Name _____ Date _____

Separate the set into the number of parts described by the denominator. Then shade the
number of parts described by the numerator. Complete each equation. The first one has
been done for you.

①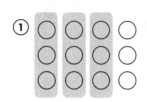

$\dfrac{3}{4}$ of 12 =   9

_____

②

$\dfrac{2}{5}$ of 20 =

_____

③

$\dfrac{4}{5}$ of 15 =

_____

④

$\dfrac{3}{4}$ of 8 =

_____

⑤

$\dfrac{3}{4}$ of 24 =

_____

⑥

$\dfrac{2}{3}$ of 21 =

_____

⑦

$\dfrac{4}{7}$ of 14 =

_____

Name _____ Date _____

Determine the fractional part of the whole number. Write the product.

① $\dfrac{2}{3}$ of 12 = _____

② $\dfrac{3}{5}$ of 20 = _____

③ $\dfrac{4}{7}$ of 21 = _____

④ $\dfrac{3}{8}$ of 16 = _____

⑤ $\dfrac{3}{4}$ of 24 = _____

⑥ $\dfrac{5}{6}$ of 30 = _____

⑦ $\dfrac{1}{2}$ of 8 = _____

⑧ $\dfrac{3}{4}$ of 32 = _____

⑨ $\dfrac{7}{8}$ of 56 = _____

⑩ $\dfrac{4}{5}$ of 45 = _____

⑪ $\dfrac{3}{10}$ of 50 = _____

⑫ $\dfrac{2}{9}$ of 27 = _____

⑬ $\dfrac{1}{8}$ of 40 = _____

⑭ $\dfrac{3}{4}$ of 12 = _____

⑮ $\dfrac{2}{7}$ of 49 = _____

Name _____ Date _____

Determine the fractional part of the whole number. Write the product.

① $\frac{3}{5}$ of 20 = _____

② $\frac{2}{7}$ of 21 = _____

③ $\frac{3}{4}$ of 40 = _____

④ $\frac{2}{6}$ of 24 = _____

⑤ $\frac{3}{5}$ of 35 = _____

⑥ $\frac{1}{3}$ of 18 = _____

⑦ $\frac{1}{2}$ of 14 = _____

⑧ $\frac{3}{4}$ of 28 = _____

⑨ $\frac{3}{8}$ of 40 = _____

⑩ $\frac{1}{4}$ of 24 = _____

⑪ $\frac{1}{7}$ of 42 = _____

⑫ $\frac{5}{8}$ of 24 = _____

⑬ $\frac{3}{5}$ of 15 = _____

⑭ $\frac{3}{4}$ of 32 = _____

⑮ $\frac{3}{9}$ of 81 = _____

Name _____ Date _____

In these sets of equal fractions, the first denominator is either 10 or 100.
Find the missing numerators.

① $\dfrac{1}{10} = \dfrac{}{100}$

② $\dfrac{3}{100} = \dfrac{}{100}$

③ $\dfrac{6}{10} = \dfrac{}{100}$

④ $\dfrac{3}{10} = \dfrac{}{100}$

⑤ $\dfrac{7}{10} = \dfrac{}{100}$

⑥ $\dfrac{6}{100} = \dfrac{}{100}$

⑦ $\dfrac{4}{10} = \dfrac{}{100}$

⑧ $\dfrac{13}{100} = \dfrac{}{100}$

⑨ $\dfrac{9}{10} = \dfrac{}{100}$

⑩ $\dfrac{1}{100} = \dfrac{}{100}$

⑪ $\dfrac{8}{10} = \dfrac{}{100}$

⑫ $\dfrac{2}{10} = \dfrac{}{100}$

⑬ $\dfrac{7}{100} = \dfrac{}{100}$

⑭ $\dfrac{5}{10} = \dfrac{}{100}$

⑮ $\dfrac{16}{100} = \dfrac{}{100}$

Name _____ Date _____

Express the fractions in terms of equal denominators. Add to find the sum.

① $\dfrac{3}{10} + \dfrac{6}{100} =$ ② $\dfrac{7}{100} + \dfrac{5}{10} =$

③ $\dfrac{9}{100} + \dfrac{4}{10} =$ ④ $\dfrac{6}{10} + \dfrac{8}{100} =$

⑤ $\dfrac{8}{10} + \dfrac{13}{100} =$ ⑥ $\dfrac{23}{100} + \dfrac{4}{10} =$

⑦ $\dfrac{29}{100} + \dfrac{4}{10} =$ ⑧ $\dfrac{7}{100} + \dfrac{4}{10} =$

⑨ $\dfrac{8}{10} + \dfrac{14}{100} =$ ⑩ $\dfrac{5}{10} + \dfrac{37}{100} =$

Name _____ Date _____

Express the fractions in terms of equal denominators. Add to find the sum.

① $\dfrac{7}{10} + \dfrac{11}{100} =$

② $\dfrac{43}{100} + \dfrac{4}{10} =$

③ $\dfrac{8}{10} + \dfrac{15}{100} =$

④ $\dfrac{7}{10} + \dfrac{2}{100} =$

⑤ $\dfrac{72}{100} + \dfrac{2}{10} =$

⑥ $\dfrac{3}{10} + \dfrac{5}{100} =$

⑦ $\dfrac{54}{100} + \dfrac{2}{10} =$

⑧ $\dfrac{6}{100} + \dfrac{3}{10} =$

⑨ $\dfrac{5}{10} + \dfrac{38}{100} =$

⑩ $\dfrac{2}{10} + \dfrac{61}{100} =$

Name _____ Date _____

Shade the model to show the given decimal.

① 0.7

② 0.3

③ 0.9

④ 0.4

⑤ 0.8

⑥ 0.1

⑦ 0.23

⑧ 0.04

⑨ 0.69

⑩ 0.98

⑪ 0.51

⑫ 0.15

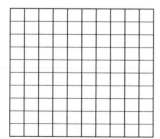
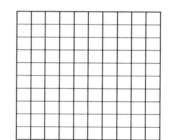
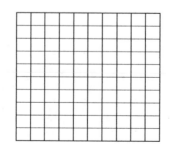
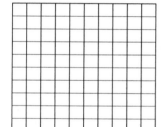
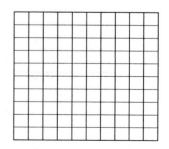
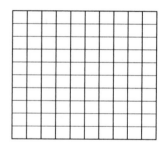

Name _____ Date _____

Look at each model and write the value of the decimal.

① _____

② _____

③ _____

④ _____

⑤ _____

⑥ _____

⑦ _____

⑧ _____

⑨ _____

⑩ _____

⑪ _____

⑫ _____

Name _____ Date _____

Look at each model and write the value of the decimal.

① _____

② _____

③ _____

④ _____

⑤ _____

⑥ _____

⑦ _____

⑧ _____

⑨ _____

⑩ _____

⑪ _____

⑫ _____

Name _____ Date _____

Rewrite the decimals so that the ones places are lined up. Circle the ones places. The first one has been done for you.

① 134.07   2.618

$$13\boxed{4}.07$$
$$\boxed{2}.618$$

② 53   2.09

③ 0.01   29

④ 62.8   5.34

⑤ 2.573   4.21

⑥ 52.07   7.3

⑦ 2.91   3.05

⑧ 5.243   62.14

⑨ 57.35   2.203

⑩ 13.3   61.39

⑪ 1500.4   36

⑫ 1207   20.7

⑬ 15   3.92

⑭ 0.931   54

⑮ 52.37   5.237

Name _____ Date _____

Circle the place that determines which number is greater. Then compare each pair of decimals. Use <, >, or =.

① 2.461
2.468

2.461 ___ 2.468

② 72.08
71.99

72.08 ___ 71.99

③ 5.031
6.144

5.031 ___ 6.144

④ 286.3
279.4

286.3 ___ 279.4

⑤ 3,284.61
3,273.88

3,284.61 ___ 3,273.88

⑥ 1.05
1.04

1.05 ___ 1.04

⑦ 5.32
5.17

5.32 ___ 5.17

⑧ 34.295
34.172

34.295 ___ 34.172

⑨ 0.004
0.101

0.004 ___ 0.101

Name _____ Date _____

Compare each pair of decimals. Use <, >, or =.

① 4.251 ___ 41.40

② 2.609 ___ 26.09

③ 534.2 ___ 534.2

④ 87 ___ 8.95

⑤ 6 ___ 0.17

⑥ 54.32 ___ 54.23

⑦ 7.706 ___ 7.706

⑧ 8.254 ___ 8.26

⑨ 700 ___ 59.425

⑩ 50.15 ___ 49.98

⑪ 814.6 ___ 8.999

⑫ 0.4 ___ 0.19

Name _____ Date _____

How many squares are being covered by each rectangle?

①

_____ squares

②

_____ squares

③

_____ squares

④

_____ squares

⑤

_____ squares

⑥

_____ squares

Name _____ Date _____

How many square units is each rectangle?

①

_____ squares

②

_____ squares

③

_____ squares

④

_____ squares

⑤

_____ squares

⑥

_____ squares

25 Common Core Math Lessons for the Interactive Whiteboard: Grade 4 © 2014 by Steve Wyborney, Scholastic Teaching Resources

Name _____ Date _____

Determine the area of each rectangle and write it on the blank line.

①   5 cm

3 cm

_____

②   9 ft

4 ft

_____

③   6 m

9 m

_____

④   16 cm

8 cm

_____

⑤   9 yds

9 yds

_____

⑥   9 in.

13 in.

_____

⑦   9 m

14 m

_____

⑧   17 m

8 m

_____

⑨   19 cm

9 cm

_____

⑩   5 yds

8 yds

_____

Name _____ Date _____

Extend the arc to draw a complete circle.

①
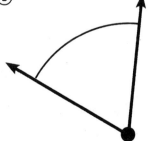

②
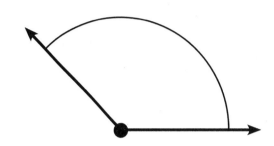

③

④
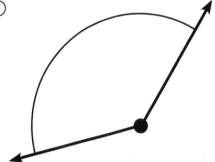

⑤
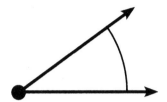

⑥
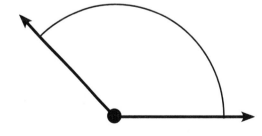

Name _____ Date _____

Label the measure of each angle.

① _____

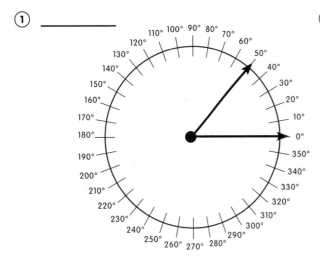

② _____

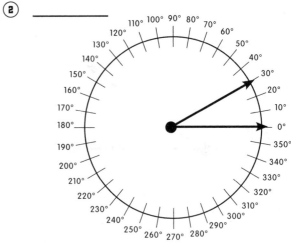

③ _____

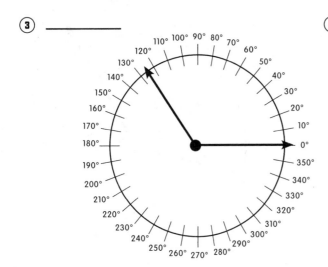

④ _____

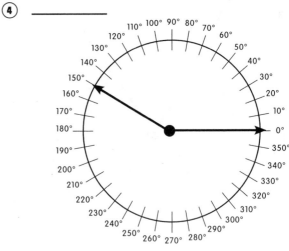

⑤ _____

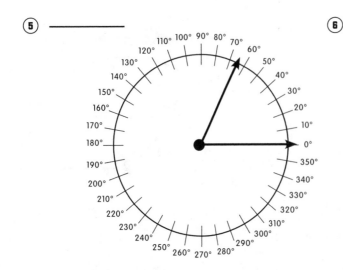

⑥ _____

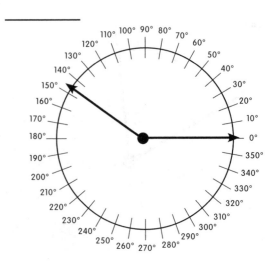

25 Common Core Math Lessons for the Interactive Whiteboard: Grade 4 © 2014 by Steve Wyborney, Scholastic Teaching Resources

Name _____ Date _____

Label the measure of each angle. The angle measurements are listed below.

10°, 30°, 60°, 90°, 110°, 140°, 165°, 180°

① _____

② _____

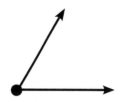

③ _____

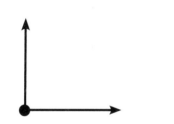

④ _____

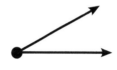

⑤ _____

⑥ _____

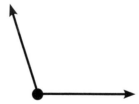

⑦ _____

⑧ _____

Name _____ Date _____

Label the measure of each angle.

① _____

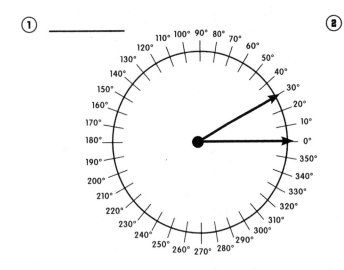

② _____

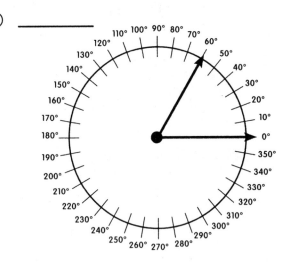

③ _____

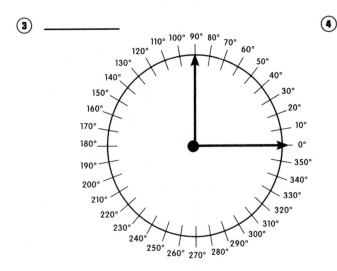

④ _____

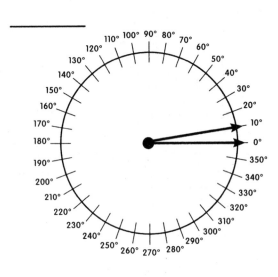

⑤ _____

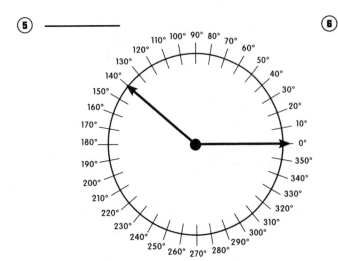

⑥ _____

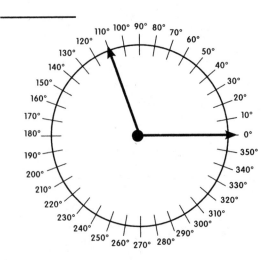

Sketching Angles: B

Name _____ Date _____

Draw the specified angle.

①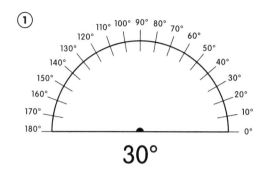
30°

②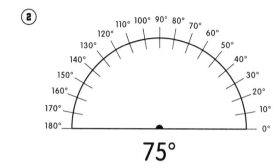
75°

③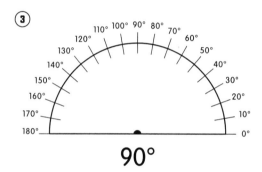
90°

④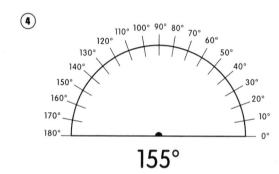
155°

⑤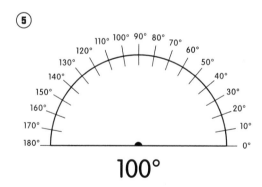
100°

⑥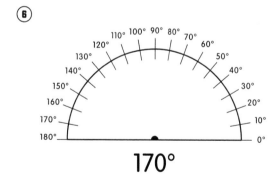
170°

⑦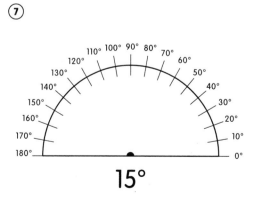
15°

⑧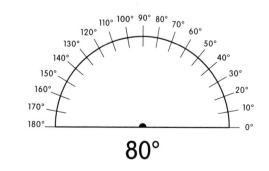
80°

Name _____ Date _____

Use the geometric shape to sketch the specified angle.

①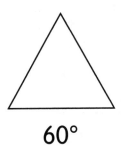
60°

②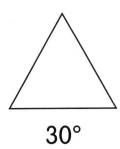
30°

③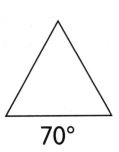
70°

④
90°

⑤
45°

⑥
100°

⑦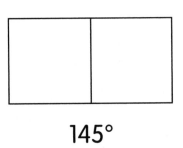
145°

⑧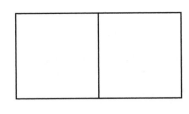
160°

Name _____ Date _____

**Use a ruler and a pencil to continue drawing each line in both directions. Label each pair of
lines as "Parallel" or "Not Parallel."**

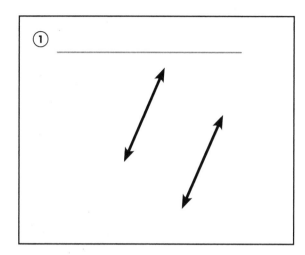

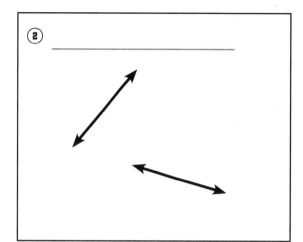

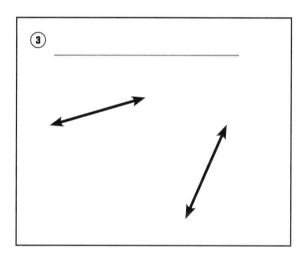

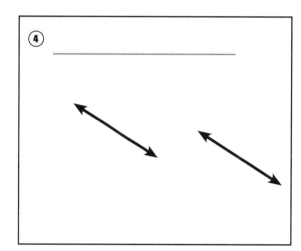

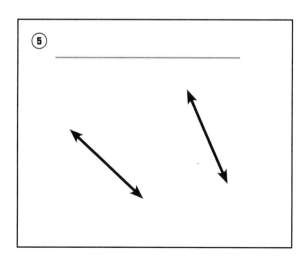

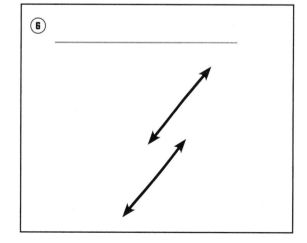

85

Parallel Lines and Parallelograms: B

Name _____ Date _____

Circle the pairs of lines that are parallel.

①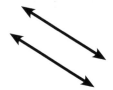

②

③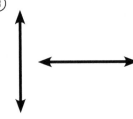

④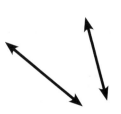

⑤

⑥

⑦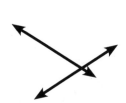

⑧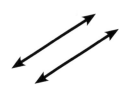

⑨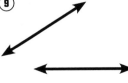

⑩

⑪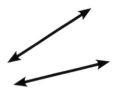

⑫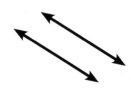

86

Name _____ Date _____

Shade the shapes that are parallelograms.

①
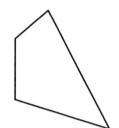

②
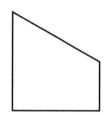

③
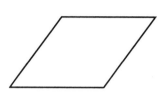

④
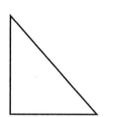

⑤
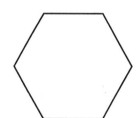

⑥
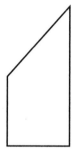

⑦
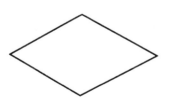

⑧
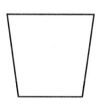

⑨
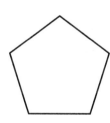

⑩

⑪

⑫

Name _____ Date _____

Each of these shapes has at least one line of symmetry. Draw a line of symmetry in each shape. The first one has been done for you.

①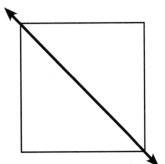

②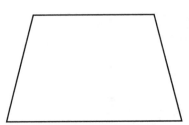

③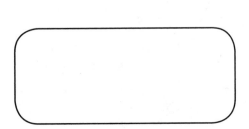

④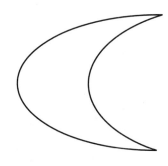

⑤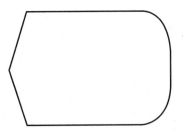

⑥

⑦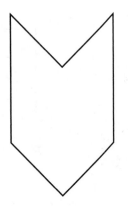

⑧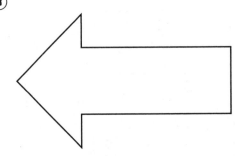

88

Name _____ Date _____

Shade the shapes that have line symmetry. Draw a line of symmetry in those shapes.

①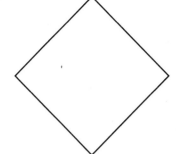

②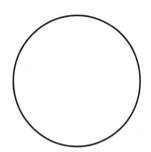

③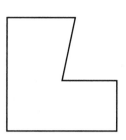

④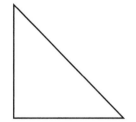

⑤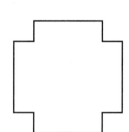

⑥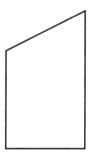

⑦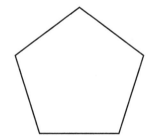

⑧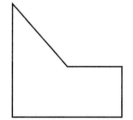

⑨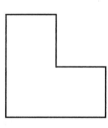

⑩

⑪

⑫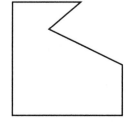

Name _____ Date _____

Each of the shapes below is missing exactly one half of the whole shape. A line of symmetry is shown. Complete the shape so that it has line symmetry.

①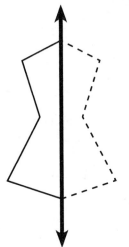

②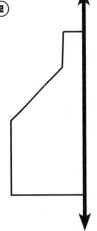

③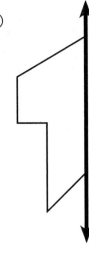

④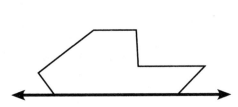

⑤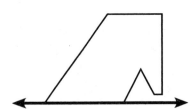

⑥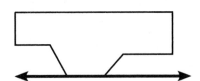

⑦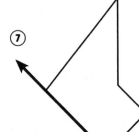

⑧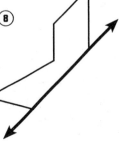

⑨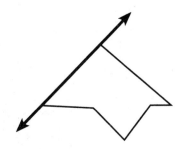

Understanding Multiplication

A (p. 16): **1.** 56 **2.** 40 **3.** 27 **4.** 42 **5.** 40 **6.** 15

B (p. 17):

1.

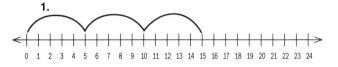

2.

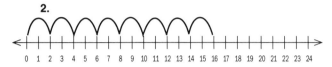

3.

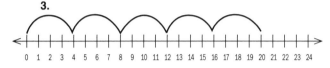

4.

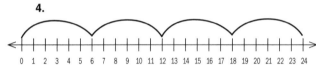

5.

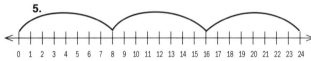

6.

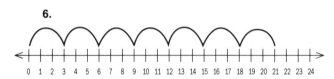

C (p. 18): **1.** 15 **2.** 18 **3.** 28 **4.** 64 **5.** 9 **6.** 9 **7.** 28 **8.** 30
9. 90 **10.** 70 **11.** 3 **12.** 32 **13.** 56 **14.** 48 **15.** 54

Divisibility Test for 3

A (p. 19): **1.** No **2.** Yes, 1 **3.** No **4.** Yes, 1 **5.** No **6.** No
7. Yes, 2 **8.** Yes, 2

B (p. 20): **1.** 7, no **2.** 15, yes **3.** 11, no **4.** 9, yes
5. 17, no **6.** 15, yes **7.** 15, yes **8.** 21, yes

C (p. 21): **1.** No **2.** No **3.** Yes **4.** No **5.** Yes **6.** No
7. No **8.** Yes **9.** No **10.** Yes **11.** No **12.** Yes **13.** Yes
14. No **15.** No

Finding Factor Pairs

A (p. 22): **1.** 1 × 6, 2 × 3 **2.** 1 × 8, 2 × 4 **3.** 1 × 9, 3 × 3
4. 1 × 10, 2 × 5 **5.** 1 × 12, 2 × 6, 3 × 4, **6.** 1 × 14, 2 × 7
7. 1 × 15, 3 × 5 **8.** 1 × 16, 2 × 8, 4 × 4

B (p. 23): **1.** 1 × 18, 2 × 9, 3 × 6 **2.** 1 × 20, 2 × 10, 4 × 5
3. 1 × 21, 3 × 7 **4.** 1 × 24, 2 × 12, 3 × 8, 4 × 6
5. 1 × 27, 3 × 9 **6.** 1 × 30, 2 × 15, 3 × 10, 5 × 6
7. 1 × 33, 3 × 11 **8.** 1 × 36, 2 × 18, 3 × 12, 4 × 9, 6 × 6

C (p. 24): **1.** True **2.** True **3.** False **4.** True **5.** False
6. True **7.** True **8.** True **9.** False **10.** False **11.** False
12. True

Place Value & Expanded Form

A (p. 25): **2.** 50,000 **3.** 900,000 **4.** 6 **5.** 30,000
6. 400,000 **7.** 700 **8.** 1,000 **9.** 200,000 **10.** 40,000
11. 600 **12.** 40

B (p. 26): **1.** 400 + 90 + 5 **2.** 3,000 + 900 + 10 + 6
3. 7,000 + 500 + 30 + 8 **4.** 600 + 30 + 7 **5.** 20,000 +
3,000 + 800 + 10 + 6 **6.** 70,000 + 400 + 80 + 1
7. 80,000 + 4,000 + 300 **8.** 700,000 + 30,000 + 8,000 +
200 + 60 + 4 **9.** 500,000 + 10,000 + 9,000 + 300 + 6
10. 400,000 + 60,000 + 3,000 + 700 + 40 + 5

C (p. 27): **1.** 378 **2.** 2,352 **3.** 56,492 **4.** 307,064
5. 67,005 **6.** 5,536 **7.** 230,098 **8.** 912,543 **9.** 85,239
10. 53,694

Comparing Numbers

A (p. 28): **1.** < **2.** = **3.** < **4.** > **5.** = **6.** > **7.** > **8.** >
9. = **10.** < **11.** > **12.** < **13.** < **14.** < **15.** >

B (p. 29): **1.** Tens, > **2.** Ones, > **3.** Thousands, <
4. Hundreds, > **5.** Thousands, > **6.** Ten thousands, <
7. Ten thousands, > **8.** Tens, > **9.** Thousands, <

C (p. 30): **1.** > **2.** > **3.** = **4.** < **5.** < **6.** < **7.** > **8.** >
9. = **10.** >

Rounding Whole Numbers

A (p. 31): **1.** 8 **2.** 1 **3.** 8 **4.** 6 **5.** 0 **6.** 3 **7.** 4 **8.** 4 **9.** 3
10. 0 **11.** 9 **12.** 5 **13.** 7 **14.** 5 **15.** 5

B (p. 32): **1.** 34 **2.** 231 **3.** 1,730 **4.** 36 **5.** 135 **6.** 2,935
7. 5 **8.** 69 **9.** 108 **10.** 5 **11.** 78 **12.** 698 **13.** 4 **14.** 23
15. 3

C (p. 33): **1.** 520 **2.** 6,290 **3.** 15,290 **4.** 600 **5.** 251,400
6. 16,600 **7.** 9,000 **8.** 542,000 **9.** 25,000 **10.** 60,000
11. 160,000 **12.** 70,000 **13.** 600,000 **14.** 6,300,000
15. 700,000

Adding Multi-Digit Whole Numbers

A (p. 34): **1.** 4,787 **2.** 5,867 **3.** 8,389 **4.** 6,859 **5.** 9,798
6. 8,496 **7.** 58,398 **8.** 24,695 **9.** 67,473 **10.** 39,929
11. 95,955 **12.** 86,697 **13.** 697,965 **14.** 795,686
15. 885,957

B (p. 35): **1.** 6,735 **2.** 8,812 **3.** 12,039 **4.** 5,192
5. 13,669 **6.** 7,612 **7.** 92,352 **8.** 97,614 **9.** 90,680
10. 100,618 **11.** 158,603 **12.** 135,360 **13.** 713,953
14. 752,073 **15.** 597,617

C (p. 36): **1.** 11,317 **2.** 5,577 **3.** 12,827 **4.** 10,425
5. 7,243 **6.** 11,097 **7.** 60,137 **8.** 76,994 **9.** 84,021
10. 101,657 **11.** 61,280 **12.** 147,068 **13.** 1,177,386
14. 1,044,487 **15.** 1,270,858

Subtracting Multi-Digit Whole Numbers

A (p. 37): **1.** 155 **2.** 732 **3.** 503 **4.** 314 **5.** 4,791
6. 1,061 **7.** 3,003 **8.** 16 **9.** 2,000 **10.** 11,062

11. 57,401 **12.** 32,064 **13.** 436,040 **14.** 20,130
15. 134,001
B (p. 38): **1.** 316 **2.** 681 **3.** 207 **4.** 237 **5.** 360 **6.** 549
7. 1,328 **8.** 4,445 **9.** 6,564 **10.** 17 **11.** 5,293 **12.** 1,137
13. 12,802 **14.** 24,305 **15.** 3,254
C (p. 39): **1.** 337 **2.** 507 **3.** 177 **4.** 127 **5.** 43 **6.** 26
7. 1,000 **8.** 505 **9.** 1,024 **10.** 1,099 **11.** 2,199
12. 6,006 **13.** 2,737 **14.** 1,596 **15.** 17,733

Multiplying Whole Numbers by a One-Digit Number
A (p. 40): **1.** 46 **2.** 15 **3.** 48 **4.** 57 **5.** 80 **6.** 355 **7.** 96
8. 249 **9.** 366 **10.** 268 **11.** 2,088 **12.** 2,109 **13.** 487
14. 1,668 **15.** 1,005
B (p. 41): **1.** 92 **2.** 310 **3.** 511 **4.** 260 **5.** 430 **6.** 117
7. 864 **8.** 3,766 **9.** 1,872 **10.** 7,866 **11.** 5,124
12. 6,592 **13.** 4,515 **14.** 5,688 **15.** 5,382
C (p. 42): **1.** 320 **2.** 438 **3.** 765 **4.** 2,728 **5.** 395
6. 5,719 **7.** 2,810 **8.** 2,032 **9.** 2,046 **10.** 6,344
11. 31,328 **12.** 12,102 **13.** 15,172 **14.** 56,588
15. 47,712

Multiplying 2-Digit Numbers by 2-Digit Numbers
A (p. 43): **1.** 238 **2.** 247 **3.** 234 **4.** 225
B (p. 44): **1.** 676 **2.** 2,562 **3.** 5,913 **4.** 4,544
5. 1,974 **6.** 3,276 **7.** 5,229 **8.** 3,692 **9.** 1,408
C (p. 45): **1.** 2,240 **2.** 2,407 **3.** 4,134 **4.** 1,363
5. 1,116 **6.** 1,767 **7.** 2,773 **8.** 2,044 **9.** 8,084

Equal Fractions
A (p. 46): **1.** ×5 **2.** ×8 **3.** ×3 **4.** ÷3 **5.** ×8 **6.** ÷7
7. ×3 **8.** ÷7 **9.** ÷9 **10.** ×8 **11.** ÷6 **12.** ×2 **13.** ÷10
14. ×3 **15.** ÷9
B (p. 47): **1.** 8 **2.** 18 **3.** 20 **4.** 18 **5.** 72 **6.** 21 **7.** 5
8. 7 **9.** 5 **10.** 3 **11.** 5 **12.** 3 **13.** 36 **14.** 36 **15.** 5
C (p. 48): **1.** 1 **2.** 20 **3.** 63 **4.** 9 **5.** 10 **6.** 6 **7.** 56
8. 2 **9.** 8 **10.** 81 **11.** 4 **12.** 14 **13.** 25 **14.** 7 **15.** 16

Comparing Fractions
A (p. 49): **1.** < **2.** < **3.** < **4.** > **5.** < **6.** > **7.** = **8.** <
9. = **10.** > **11.** > **12.** > **13.** > **14.** < **15.** <
B (p. 50): **1.** < **2.** < **3.** < **4.** = **5.** > **6.** < **7.** = **8.** >
9. < **10.** = **11.** < **12.** < **13.** < **14.** > **15.** <
C (p. 51): **1.** < **2.** = **3.** = **4.** < **5.** = **6.** < **7.** < **8.** =
9. < **10.** > **11.** > **12.** > **13.** < **14.** < **15.** >

Comparing to Benchmark Fractions
A (p. 52): **1.** < **2.** < **3.** < **4.** > **5.** < **6.** > **7.** > **8.** >
9. > **10.** > **11.** < **12.** >
B (p. 53): **1.** < **2.** > **3.** = **4.** < **5.** > **6.** = **7.** < **8.** <
9. < **10.** = **11.** > **12.** <
C (p. 54): **1.** = **2.** < **3.** > **4.** < **5.** = **6.** > **7.** = **8.** >
9. < **10.** < **11.** > **12.** <

Adding & Subtracting Fractions
A (p. 55): **1.** 3/5 **2.** 7/8 **3.** 4/10 **4.** 5/5 **5.** 3/3 **6.** 2/4

7. 7/8 **8.** 4/10 **9.** 5/8 **10.** 6/7 **11.** 3/4 **12.** 7/9 **13.** 9/8
14. 4/3 **15.** 5/9
B (p. 56): **1.** 2/10 **2.** 4/8 **3.** 2/6 **4.** 0 **5.** 2/4 **6.** 2/4
7. 5/8 **8.** 2/10 **9.** 5/8 **10.** 4/7 **11.** 2/4 **12.** 3/9 **13.** 4/8
14. 1/3 **15.** 7/9
C (p. 57): **1.** 1/4 **2.** 8/10 **3.** 1/9 **4.** 10/8 **5.** 4/5 **6.** 1/4
7. 2/8 **8.** 3/9 **9.** 9/10 **10.** 3/8 **11.** 7/8 **12.** 2/10 **13.** 3/7
14. 3/5 **15.** 3/3

Mixed Numbers to Improper Fractions
A (p. 58): **1.** 3 1/4 **2.** 1 4/6 **3.** 5 1/3 **4.** 3 1/2 **5.** 2 3/4
6. 2 1/4
B (p. 59): **1.** 34/4 **2.** 7/2 **3.** 21/8 **4.** 11/10 **5.** 23/5
6. 37/7 **7.** 11/2 **8.** 17/6 **9.** 25/8 **10.** 14/3 **11.** 19/5
12. 25/6 **13.** 27/10 **14.** 29/9 **15.** 28/5
C (p. 60): **1.** 15/4 **2.** 51/10 **3.** 11/5 **4.** 19/4 **5.** 31/5
6. 17/2 **7.** 23/3 **8.** 8/5 **9.** 23/8 **10.** 21/5 **11.** 11/4
12. 67/10 **13.** 9/5 **14.** 13/4 **15.** 59/8

Understanding Fractions as Multiples of Unit Fractions
A (p. 61): **2.** 4/6 = 1/6 + 1/6 + 1/6 + 1/6 **3.** 3/4 = 1/4 + 1/4
+ 1/4 **4.** 4/8 = 1/8 + 1/8 + 1/8 + 1/8 **5.** 5/8 = 1/8 + 1/8 +
1/8 + 1/8 + 1/8 **6.** 2/3 = 1/3 + 1/3 **7.** 5/6 = 1/6 + 1/6 + 1/6
+ 1/6 + 1/6 **8.** 3/6 = 1/6 + 1/6 + 1/6
B (p. 62): **2.** 3/7 = 1/7 + 1/7 + 1/7 **3.** 2/3 = 1/3 + 1/3
4. 5/8 = 1/8 + 1/8 + 1/8 + 1/8 + 1/8 **5.** 3/4 = 1/4 + 1/4 +
1/4 **6.** 5/5 = 1/5 + 1/5 + 1/5 + 1/5 + 1/5 **7.** 3/8 = 1/8 + 1/8
+ 1/8 **8.** 2/4 = 1/4 + 1/4 **9.** 4/10 = 1/10 + 1/10 + 1/10 +
1/10 **10.** 3/5 = 1/5 + 1/5 + 1/5 **11.** 5/9 = 1/9 + 1/9 + 1/9
+ 1/9 + 1/9 **12.** 4/4 = 1/4 + 1/4 + 1/4 + 1/4 **13.** 2/6 = 1/6
+ 1/6 **14.** 4/7 = 1/7 + 1/7 + 1/7 + 1/7
C (p. 63): **2.** 3/8 **3.** 7/10 **4.** 2 **5.** 1/8 **6.** 5/9 **7.** 9/10
8. 3/5 **9.** 6 **10.** 1/7 **11.** 5/6 **12.** 1/8

Multiplying Fractions by Whole Numbers
A (p. 64): **2.** 8 **3.** 12 **4.** 6 **5.** 18 **6.** 14 **7.** 8
B (p. 65): **1.** 8 **2.** 12 **3.** 12 **4.** 6 **5.** 18 **6.** 25 **7.** 4
8. 24 **9.** 49 **10.** 36 **11.** 15 **12.** 6 **13.** 5 **14.** 9 **15.** 14
C (p. 66): **1.** 12 **2.** 6 **3.** 30 **4.** 8 **5.** 21 **6.** 6 **7.** 7 **8.** 21
9. 15 **10.** 6 **11.** 6 **12.** 15 **13.** 9 **14.** 24 **15.** 27

Adding Two Fractions With Denominators 10 and 100
A (p. 67): **1.** 10 **2.** 3 **3.** 60 **4.** 30 **5.** 70 **6.** 6 **7.** 40
8. 13 **9.** 90 **10.** 1 **11.** 80 **12.** 20 **13.** 7 **14.** 50 **15.** 16
B (p. 68): **1.** 36/100 **2.** 57/100 **3.** 49/100 **4.** 68/100
5. 93/100 **6.** 63/100 **7.** 69/100 **8.** 47/100 **9.** 94/100
10. 87/100
C (p. 69): **1.** 81/100 **2.** 83/100 **3.** 95/100 **4.** 72/100
5. 92/100 **6.** 35/100 **7.** 74/100 **8.** 36/100 **9.** 88/100
10. 81/100

Reading Decimal Models
A (p. 70): Answers will vary.
B (p. 71): **1.** 0.4 **2.** 0.9 **3.** 0.6 **4.** 0.1 **6.** 0.8 **6.** 0.2